Audible Signs

Audible Signs

Essays from a Musical Ground

Michael Alec Rose

continuum

2010
The Continuum International Publishing Group
80 Maiden Lane, New York, NY 10038
The Tower Building, 11 York Road, London SE1 7NX

www.continuumbooks.com

Permission to use the digital image of the painting *Maddelena penitente*
by Michelangelo Merisi da Caravaggio (Galleria Doria Pamphilj, Rome):
ADP/ALINARI Archives, Florence.
Permission to use the digital image of the drawing *Gottes Verheisung
an Abraham* by Rembrandt Harmenszoon van Rijn (Inv. nr. 1327):
Rembrandt. Die Dresdner Zeichnungen 2004, bearb. von Christian
Dittrich und Thomas Ketelsen, Staatliche Kunstsammlungen Dresden,
Kupferstich-Kabinett, Köln 2004, S. 200f., Nr. 114.
Translation of "Nimm sie hin denn, diese Lieder" by Alois Jeitteles,
copyright © 1997 by Lynn Thompson: l-thompson@wiu.edu
Translation of "Nänie" by Friedrich von Schiller, copyright © by Emily
Ezust, from The Lied and Art Song Texts Page: http://www.lieder.net/

Library of Congress Cataloging-in-Publication Data
Rose, Michael Alec, 1959–
Audible signs : essays from a musical ground / by Michael Alec Rose.
   p. cm.
   ISBN-13: 978-1-4411-4326-6 (hardcover : alk. paper)
   ISBN-10: 1-4411-4326-2 (hardcover : alk. paper)
   ISBN-13: 978-1-4411-8050-6 (pbk. : alk. paper)
   ISBN-10: 1-4411-8050-8 (pbk. : alk. paper) 1. Music—Philosophy and
aesthetics. I. Title.
   ML3800.R59 2010
   781.1'7—dc22   2010004153

ISBN: 978-1-4411-4326-6 (Hardback)
       978-1-4411-8050-6 (Paperback)

Typeset by Pindar NZ, Auckland, New Zealand
Printed in the United States of America by Thomson-Shore, Inc

Contents

Preface
and Hypothesis

At the start of every semester, I tell my students that two things (among others) help a person to flourish and have fun in the world and, to begin with, in my courses: first, to develop and to share ideas, however strange they may be — not *opinions*, but *ideas*, founded upon vivid evidence; and second, not merely to be ready for others to dispute your ideas, but to welcome such disputation as the springboard for civility and mutual understanding. Some undergraduates are naturally more inclined to take this advice than others. I tend to spend more of my hours with those who are less so, just as the revivalist preacher takes more time with the doubting than with the faithful.

For sure, my own Jewish tradition is founded on disputation, in the Talmudic arguments among the rabbis. In this book I am sometimes immoderately disputatious, most forcefully against the book, *The Rest Is Noise*, by the brilliant music journalist Alex Ross. The argument I have with Ross ought to be taken as a readable sign of my abiding respect for his achievement. So did the rabbis show their love and gratitude for each other, by duking it out over this or that point of Jewish law.

My favorite *midrash* — a Talmudic story designed to clarify, enrich, and complicate the literal text of the Bible — is the one in which the disputation among rabbis and their students over a passage of Torah becomes so heated that God decides to intervene and resolve the argument. The divine light irradiates the study hall and God's voice is heard by the awestruck disputants: "My children, you have shown such superb devotion to My Word that I will help you understand what I meant, just this once." A silence; then, in one thundering voice, everyone in the room shouts back, "Shut up!"

I have composed *Audible Signs* in the spirit of this *midrash*: not to offer up any sacrifices to singular truth for the sake of music, but to engage in "the asking mystery," which philosopher Michael Gelven identifies as the heart of all worthy human endeavor. I thank all my Vanderbilt students for their tough questions over the years, especially my dear friends Lee Hallman, Russell Johnston and Cherie Snyder, whose questions have been the most illuminating and affectionate — which is to say the most vexing and disputatious.

Let the disputations begin!

Here's a hypothesis for you:

In the Western tradition, composers innovate their technical resources from generation to generation in order to account more faithfully for the range and complexity of human feeling. They take their musical risks in order to establish a broader sovereignty of expression that more closely approaches the lived and embodied texture of emotional experience.

Clarification is immediately called for: the hypothesis seeks to describe the *spirit* of composers as they fashion their innovations. It does not propose that composers actually succeed in this venture. Such a claim would commit the double error of teleology ("there is a goal to music history") and ideology ("this goal is a desirable consummation, devoutly to be wished").

We do not have to be either teleological or ideological to entertain the possibility that composers have always striven to make their music a more accurate reflection of their own and their fellow human beings' psychological reality than the music of their predecessors. Intentionality need not be a fallacy. Only a muddle-headed spirit and a flawed body of evidence make ideas fallacious.

Here is how the hypothesis might work:

In the Middle Ages, composers developed more and more complex polyphonic notation (composed scores, indicating different voices singing at the same time) in order to celebrate the greater glory of God. This brand-new sonority worked hand in prayerful hand with the brand-new, "polyphonic" architecture of Gothic cathedrals. At the same time, secular polyphony presented composers with a dizzying proliferation of textual perspectives, in keeping with the Church's and Court's hierarchy of mind over matter.

(We interrupt this hypothesis for an important historical bulletin! Already the vast range of medieval music defeats any teleological view: there are monophonic Gregorian chants and troubadour chansons — concurrent with the invention of composed polyphony — whose melodic beauties are equal to, or surpass, any subsequent development in music. That's why I emphasize the point that my hypothesis treats the *subjective* spirit of Western music's development: what composers *themselves* hoped to achieve.)

In the Renaissance, composers evolved a more equal dispensation of singing voices, allowing an impressively *humane* glorification of God or Eros to arise out of the more sensuous polyphony. To these innovators, there was no base matter, no unseemly dissonance, that could not be turned into aural gold.

In the Baroque, composers polarized the singing voice from its accompaniment in order to invoke the rhetorical texture of ancient Athenian tragedy. This new ground — opera and oratorio — made both Greek myth and the Holy Bible available to dramatic musical expression. This polarization also took shape in instrumental music, where the concerto dramatized music to the same degree as its vocal counterparts.

During the Classic period, composers innovated sonata form in order to project more gracefully the internal contrast of characters at work in the human heart and on the operatic stage. The ingenious mustering of a dramatic ensemble preoccupied the structuring of symphonic and chamber music as surely as it did opera.

In the Romantic era, composers dissolved the symmetrical structures of Classic form so as to empower a wider, wilder, more immediate contrast of emotions, unleashing the heroic unpredictability and Promethean waywardness of the human psyche. Ironically, the tonal relations among chords and keys became more *symmetrical* than in the Classic era, whose diatonic asymmetry gave way to chromatic circularity. This transfer of constructive artifice from Classic depth to Romantic surface marked a radical shift of psychological perspective from grounded certainty to an anxious suspension thereof.

In the modernist epoch, composers both inveighed against and intensified the Romantic *hubris* of heroic self-expression, exacting a toll on their listeners still almost impossible to pay after a century's worth of listening. The modernists' generally dark psychic reality is of a piece with the twentieth century's overall darkness, faithful to its discordant history. The impossibility of upholding a teleology of historical progress in the face of unending human misery, cruelty and folly — articulated so forcefully by Schoenberg in *Moses und Aron* and Stravinsky in *The Rake's Progress* — makes a mockery of the hardened teleology of *musical* progress upheld by these selfsame Olympian modernists.

Once again, it is the *spirit* of composers' innovations, in whatever era, that matters largely in taking a full and accurate measure of their achievements, especially their breakthrough redefinitions of musical beauty. Schoenberg and Stravinsky are unsurpassed in this regard. For the modernists, teleology was everything. The totalizing projection of a perfect world of twelve-tone music or Apollonian detachment makes both Schoenberg and Stravinsky uncomfortably close in spirit to their respective compatriots Hitler and Stalin, and infinitely removed from them in practice. Thank goodness great composers are not the legislators of the world.

I am ready to admit that my hypothesis about the process (*not* progress!) of innovation throughout music history is impossible to prove, as is every other idea I hypothesize in this book. What I hope to do is give convincing evidence for these ideas through *the experience of music itself.** I would like nothing better, dear reader, than for you to dispute with me. Only then could my *hypothesis* be ready for promotion to *thesis*, as a bill must come before Congress before it can be passed into law. By a neat coincidence, *thesis* is the ancient technical term for a strong beat in music, towards which an unstable *anacrusis* (the preceding upbeat) tends. *Audible Signs* is my *anacrusis*, hoping for you to complete its rhythmic impetus.

---

* without footnotes (this is the only one in the book).

Acknowledgments

Thanks to:

Four Roses and a fifth — Maman, Lewis, Suzi, Faina, Kenny — and the *ganze mishpucha*.

The speed-dial crew: Bill Rosenthal, Brian Peterson, Maria Lambros, Mark van Gorder, Perry Perretz, and Marc Soble.

The Pagods, *et alia*: Jeremy Pick, Paul Ousley, Tim Riley, Pat Crumpley, Joe Patchen, Eric Davidson, Robert May, Tony Boutté, and Donald Sloan.

My three graces: Kathryn Plummer, Elizabeth Anderson, and Marianne Osiel.

My foremost teachers: Isaac Wall, Leonard Murphy, Joan Cobb, Ivan Caine, Robert Carl, Richard Wernick, George Crumb, Jay Reise, Larry Bernstein, Norman Smith, Samuel Adler, John Harbison, and Dennis Lee.

Isadore Rose, George Rochberg, Guy Davenport, Kenneth Schermerhorn (*aleyhem hashalom*).

All my Nashville pals, who have managed so patiently their unmanageable colleague: Chris Teal, Connie Heard, John Kochanowski, Felix Wang, Carolyn Huebl, Grace Bahng, Craig Nies, Mark and Amy Jarman, A. -J. Levine, Jay Geller, Jack

Sasson, John and Trisha Johns, Del Sawyer, Mark Wait, Jane Kirchner, Cynthia Cyrus, John Lachs, John Compton, Leonard Folgarait, Bev Asbury, Michael Bess, Michael Hodges, Michael Kurek, Michael Slayton, Michael Hime, Stan Link, Carl Smith, Douglas Lee, Greg Barz, Jim Lovensheimer, Joy Calico, Melanie Lowe, Dale Cockrell, Carl Johnson, Roger Wiesmeyer, Mark Cianciolo, Don Hart, Kris Wilkinson, Carol Dunne, Carol Elliott, Ann Street, Anne Roos, Ron Roth, John Eley, and Donna Scott.

My UK friends: Peter Sheppard Skærved, Aaron Shorr, Malene Skaerved, Jim Aitchison, Neil Heyde, David Gorton, Margaret Otho-Briggs, Colin Squire, Mim and Peter Umney-Gray, Richard Dalby, and Ian Phillips.

My agent, Brian Romer, who sweetly slapped my wrist.

My editor, David Barker, who gave me a free hand.

Maggie and Izzy.

This is for you, Joanna, with *aleph* love, with *taf* love

A Note on Recordings

With the single exception of my own Halloween overture, all the music in this book can readily be purchased on iTunes or at various online CD stores. For the classical works, there are of course different recordings to choose from. I have my own favorites, including the fine recording of Mozart's "Gran Partita" on the soundtrack of *Amadeus*. Part of the fun of buying classical CDs is to read reviews of the various offerings and make your own decisions. The only recording I would insist upon is Robert Shaw's masterful rendition of *Nänie*, which features in Chapter 6.

There are several streaming audio or free download websites that exist to sell music, but also allow the patron to build up a catalogue of recordings, temporarily free of charge. As a professional composer, I am naturally obliged to urge you to support the arts and buy all the fabulous music I write about in this book.

Having said that, I also want to make my hopeful intention clear from the start: *Audible Signs* is meant to be enjoyed on its own ground, independent of any need to listen to music. If I have done my work well, the book will show you that music and ideas are always interdependent. Then you may decide to purchase the glorious stuff I rave about here. In the meantime, I hope you will take pleasure in these essays and take heart considering the habit of mind I am encouraging through them.

Chapter 1

An Intimate
Iconography of Music

A woman sits alone on a low chair, in the shadowy corner of a room.

Her jewelry is cast off onto the floor at her side, her pitcher of water catching the light with a transparency equal to her own. She is girdled round with dark and excessive drapery that trails along the floor, a dusky counterpoint to the bright pearls trailing on the other side of her. Her hair is disheveled (literally "dis-tressed"). She seems lost in thought, framed by darkness, a shaft of light coursing along the wall high above her head. She is empty-handed: her pendent head and cradling arms suggest the absence of something (someone?) she has recently seen or held or lovingly regarded. Her loneliness makes our own regard something of a scandal, an intrusion, a species of spiritual voyeurism. She is unforgettable — once seen, always to be reckoned with, a permanent fixture of our knowledge of suffering humanity.

Caravaggio has painted this image so splendidly, with such rich lights and darks (the *chiaroscuro* he famously invented), with so much compassion and inscrutable drama, that we can enjoy the beauty and simple emotion of the work without any need to

1

know "what's going on," who this woman is, or what her story may be. We can give whatever interpretation we choose to the painting and we could not be wrong about whatever we come up with. Indeed, some Caravaggio scholars refuse to assign a specific title to the painting, for there is no solid evidence that the artist ever did. *Woman Sitting* should be enough . . .

Or . . .

What if we invested every single item and aspect of the picture with iconic significance? What if everything we've already described serves as a sign of some kind? The sitting on a low chair is a sign of ritual mourning in both Christian and Jewish cultures. The shadowy corner where the woman sits is an outward sign of her state of mind, overcast with grief. The castoff jewelry and unkempt hair signal her renunciation of the vain and profane things of this world. The pitcher of water stands as a visible emblem for the unprecedented clarity of her own soul, transparent with new knowledge and life-giving insight. It is also a chilling memory of the crucial act of her life, the simple act of washing a man's feet. The girdle of dark drapery cloaks her like the shroud she so recently administered, with so much grief and remorse. The shaft of light above her head shows both the possibility and remoteness of illumination for her darkened spirit. Her lowered head and exquisitely absent lap point to a dear figure that once rested there, or could have rested there, or should have rested there. She is so alone. By intruding on her loneliness, we do not diminish it, but rather partake of it and make it our own condition. We could well be in her position; in fact, we are.

She is the Magdalene, the fallen woman, the whore, now at last fully aware of her intolerable error, now penitent to the last degree of grief at the dreadful torture and death of her Redeemer.

What is the difference between these two familiar and obvious modes of looking at a picture (among so many others) that I have set forth? Is the second, sign-laden approach superior to the first, straightforwardly descriptive one? Once we are given the "key," can we ever regain our innocence towards the picture so that we can just *look* at it and simply see a woman lost in thought in a chair? Why would we want to regain such innocence? How can we be honest about this without ironically acknowledging the fact that Mary Magdalene is the best exemplar we could hope for of an impossible desire for renewed innocence?

The network of signs in Caravaggio's *Maddelena penitente* (the painting's usual title) constitutes its *iconography*. One of the goals of art history is for students to accumulate as comprehensive an inventory of culturally shared signs as possible, so that they can "read" any image in all its iconographic complexity.

But there are dangers to the iconographic approach to art, especially the bad assumption that a painting is merely the sum of its referential parts (this is the unfortunate implication of many popular reference books on art these days). One way of understanding the urge towards abstract non-representation in modern art is to see it as the artist's liberation from the tyranny of iconographic determinism. Take a wild guess: which of the arts do you think inspired pioneering abstract painters like Kandinsky, Mondrian, and Kupka more than any other, as a model of liberated emotion and radical freedom from referential meaning?

Music, of course.

And so I embark on my journey with you to "unveil" the *iconography of music* with some trepidation, some anguish over my betrayal of modern art's defiant repudiation of the sign, some justifiable fear that you will think that I want to reduce music to a "road map" of audible signs. Nothing could be further from what I hope for in this book than such a stupefying reduction of musical sound to mere sign.

At the start of his thrilling book, *The Life of Forms in Art*, the great French art critic Henri Focillon celebrates the stubborn refusal of artistic form to be reduced to a singular meaning or definable content. His difficult language in the following passage is a dramatization of his essential point: *there is no way of simplifying art* (including his own art of aesthetic criticism). We must struggle with a work's opacity of meaning and indeterminacy of subject, which will draw us back again and again for spiritual sustenance, if we let it. Here is how Focillon puts it:

> Any likening of form to sign is a tacit admission of the conventional distinction between form and subject-matter — a distinction that may become misleading if we forget that the *fundamental content of form is a formal one* [emphasis added]. Form is never the catch-as-catch-can garment of subject-matter. No, it is the various interpretations of subject-matter that are so unstable and insecure. *As old meanings are broken down and obliterated, new meanings attach themselves to form.*

This closing, italicized emphasis is again mine, for this last sentence nicely sums up what my book aims for, through a variety of approaches: an investigation of how new meanings attach themselves to musical form through the ingenious invocation of "audible signs." In Focillon's own reckoning elsewhere in his lovely book, music serves as the exemplary art of what is "unstable and insecure." Music releases us from the oppressive presence — or willful absence — of referential image in the other arts (including the written word). Music stands as the most powerful dissolution of the "conventional distinction between form and subject-matter." In music, the sound — the form that the sound takes — *is* the subject matter, nothing more or less than that.

So why would I perversely want to show you how composers across so many centuries and historical styles have invested their music with audible signs, with just as much iconographic density as Caravaggio exerts in his Magdalene picture? The question is all the more urgent when we consider how misguided it would be to reduce Caravaggio's picture to an inventory of its iconographic content, winding up at the Magdalene story as if that were the "meaning" of the picture (I can hear Focillon shouting, "*Mais non, absolument pas!*").

There is a single, compelling answer to this question that defeats all my scruples and launches this book along its wild course: the signs are *there*, they are *audible*, they belong to a piece of music just as intimately as the visual signs attend the solitary Magdalene.

But, alas, while our "muddy vesture" of musical inattention, historical distance, and lack of cultural context "doth grossly close us in," *we cannot hear them* (these are the terms in which Shakespeare describes our mortal inability to hear the ever-present, all-abiding Music of the Spheres). This book offers a set of case studies for developing a habit of mind and a listening heart, eager, ready, and hungry to pay attention to music's audible signs and their infinitely variable transformations.

There are many different kinds of attention to pay. Mozart (presently) and Schumann (Chapter 3) invoke very different sets of sonic markers, reflecting their different historical moments and almost diametrically opposed attitudes towards their shared vocation (in short, blitheness vs. anxiety). Beethoven and the Beatles (Chapters 2 and 3) confront one and the same problem of human suffering, through glaringly contradictory resources. The entire twentieth century cannot be bound in a nutshell, but it can be more richly understood through certain "narrative signs" that apply to much of the music of that era, however discrepant in style (Chapters 3 and 4). Three great mentors of mine have a hunch about a transcendent musical spirit, which entails ("enforks"?) the summoning of demons (Chapter 5). Springsteen and Brahms both urgently address the same question of existential freedom, but with irreconcilably divergent means and agendas (Chapter 6). Rembrandt and Regina Spektor both embody an ironic image of iconoclasm (Chapter 7), each providing a clarifying lens to reveal its risks. Each chapter embraces the impossibility of constructing any systematic iconography of music; instead, every chapter offers empirical evidence for the ever-present radiance of audible signs in music of all kinds — always with the help of the allied arts.

But again, alas, so often, *we cannot hear them.* That's where I want to help, if I can.

There are at least two general kinds of audible signs that may not be audible to us without some guidance, encouragement, or shift of consciousness — or *corruption*, perhaps, in the old, ethically dangerous (to the *polis* of Athens) sense of risking Socratic attention to every last thing. Let's call the first set the "duh!" signs, the ones that are so obvious when explicated that we may not even need to talk about them. Here's an example of a "duh!" sign:

Rainbows, stars, and mountains all belong to our spiritual history of signs, spanning ages and cultures with their transcendent import. We look up to them rising above our little, wondering heads and seek from them a sign of guidance or inspiration ("I lift mine eyes to the mountains, whence cometh my help."). And so it makes sense that when we sing of rainbows, stars, and mountains, our larynxes wish to enact the aspiring movement of our imaginations. Our melodies leap a full octave, attempting to cover the distance between our earthbound selves and the skyscraping objects of our loving attention:

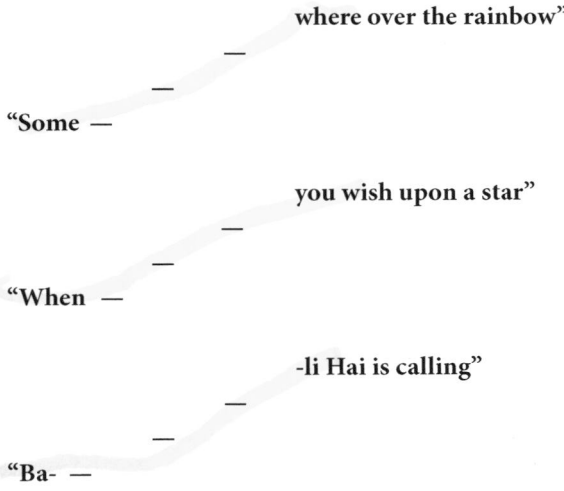

where over the rainbow"

                    —
                 —
"Some —

you wish upon a star"

                 —
              —
"When —

-li Hai is calling"

                 —
              —
"Ba- —

"Duh!" These three leaping octaves — composed by Harold Arlen for his rainbow, Leigh Harlin for his star, and Richard Rodgers for his South Pacific volcano — are such obvious "word painting," it seems trivial to mention them. But it's still a lot of fun to do so, especially in college classrooms, where a habit of paying attention to musical detail can be aided and abetted by this kind of "word-painting" interpretation. These ultra-obvious leaping octaves in the three songs are excellent instances of musical *mimesis*, an idea going back to Plato and Aristotle, whereby art works by *imitating* the images it hopes to convey. We can *feel* Dorothy's rainbow, Jiminy Cricket's star, and Bloody Mary's "Bali Hai" very vividly as their voices fly up from the low note to the high note a full octave above. But the crucial question is this: do we come to feel the emotional pull of these melodic leaps even more when we become actively conscious of them, through such an obvious, "duh!" analysis? This question fairly describes the story of my teaching life for the past quarter of a century. Generations of students have graciously assured me that *nothing* is obvious when it comes to listening to music. Therefore, I will stick by my pedagogical strategy of sharing the "duh!" audible signs with them as a point of entry for more complex investigations.

But this book is not meant to be a "duh!" book. Instead, it is about a second set of audible signs, which I want to call the "huh?" signs, the ones that are "encoded" by composers into their music with iconographic complexity and playfulness, in tacit complicity with an audience who can recognize the signs and take pleasure in their manipulations, transformations, deconstructions, and obliterations.

In league with Henri Focillon, I shout *vive l'instabilité e l'insecurité* of these audible signs. In order to celebrate how a composer plays with them and "breaks them down," we have to *learn how to hear them*. This can be difficult, in light of the era-bound, culturally specific nature of musical iconography. That's why I call them the "huh?" signs: "*Huh*? This phrase of Mozart's music is a sign of *what*? How was I expected to hear *that*?" Well, you're not expected to, unless you have some help. I hope to clear away a few "huh?"s and replace them with "WOW!"s.

Ironically, it is sometimes even more difficult to perceive the audible iconography of music going on right now. Because the music of our era is already *inside* our ear, it is altogether too familiar to us to pay any attention to. That's why it's fun to give it some attention.

It's time for a musical example. *Ohimé! Oy vey!* Caravaggio was relatively easy to talk about, especially since I am just a fan of great paintings and not professionally invested in the medium. Music makes things so hard. Believe me, after decades of teaching countless college students — many of whom have had no training whatsoever in music — how to listen to Bach, Beethoven, Berlioz, Brahms, Bartók, Boulez, and the Beatles (and that's just a few of the B's), I know just how hard it is to talk about music.

Have you noticed how the current bestselling books on music rarely attempt to recreate the experience of listening to *music itself*? They do a great job at giving the historical circumstances of a musical work or assessing music's powerful psychological effects (Alex Ross and Oliver Sacks, respectively). *But where's the B-flat, man?* Where is there any genuine effort to describe and interpret the *actual sound* of a piece of music in all its shimmering, sensuous reality? Even when Ross or Sacks makes the effort, it is always for the purpose of making some extra-musical point about history or psychology. To these writers (and perhaps to our culture at large), music seems to be meaningful only when it helps to paint a larger picture of human activity — as if listening to music were not a worthy human activity unto itself. Just look at the subtitle to Ross's book: *Listening to the Twentieth Century*. To the century, not to its music! This is a distinction that has unfortunate consequences for Ross's book (see Chapter 4).

I can sympathize with Ross and Sacks — and Levitin and Barenboim and Teachout, and just about everybody else who writes about music these days. *How to turn things around, so that history and psychology grow generously out of the attention we pay to music, rather than limit and predetermine the kind of attention we pay to it in the first place?* The problem is obvious: the moment an author starts writing about "B-flats" or "augmented sixth chords," the general reader is likely to shut down emotional shop. Of all the technical jargons in the world, the arid vocabulary of music theory is the worst kind of jargon, for it seems to be in such deplorable conflict with the expressive power of music and its exalted position in the human heart. And from the other side, it is the emotional significance of music in our lives that seems to paralyze our reasonable capacity to speak or write with any sort of lucidity or specificity about it.

Charles Rosen — one of the finest pianists and music theorists of our time, and the current doyen of public musical intellectuals — provides a depressing case in point: when he writes about classical music for *The New York Review of Books* (which he often does), he suffers from the "Goldilocks effect" I have been diagnosing: his language is either too cold with musical jargon ("celloistic timbres" and "metric modulations"), or too hot with vague and lyrical effusion, whereby a description of a trumpet solo in the *Concerto for Three Orchestras* by the austere atonal composer Elliott Carter would serve just as well for the trumpet solo in George Gershwin's ever-popular *An American in Paris*.

I do not know for certain if I can give you a musical "porridge" that is *just right*, but that is what I'm going to try to do in this book.

> *I will be the irresistible misfit*
> *who sends up over a ledge of flowers*
> *sounds no woman has ever heard —*
>
> *the one who longs to see your face*
> *framed by bougainvillea*
> *perplexed but full of charity,*

looking down at me as I finger
a nameless instrument
it took many days and nights to invent.

(from "Serenade," by Billy Collins)

After much procrastination (which can be productive in its own way), here is a musical example for you, a cultural icon (in B-flat, no less!) which will either already be familiar to you or immediately accessible to you from Netflix.

At one point in the movie *Amadeus*, Salieri picks up the score to the Adagio movement of Mozart's Serenade for Winds in B-flat Major ("Gran Partita"), K. 361, and describes the experience in an unforgettable way:

> On the page it looked nothing. The beginning simple, almost comic. Just a pulse — bassoons and basset horns — like a rusty squeezebox. Then suddenly — high above it — an oboe, a single note, hanging there unwavering, till a clarinet took over and sweetened it into a phrase of such delight! This was no composition by a performing monkey! This was a music I'd never heard. Filled with such longing, such unfulfillable longing, it had me trembling. It seemed to me that I was hearing the voice of God.

It's always the non-musicians who write best about music, about the *sound* of music and its visceral effect on us — the playwright Peter Shaffer in this case, but also the novelist Thomas Mann in his great novel *Doktor Faustus*, and innumerable poets from Homer, Shakespeare, Shelley, and Dickinson to Rilke and Yeats, Czeslaw Milosz and Denise Levertov. Of course, Shaffer has a dramatic agenda in giving Salieri voice to describe Mozart's music so vividly. In his marvelous fable, Salieri will declare war on God for having invested musical genius in such an unworthy vessel, such an obscene boy: in Mozart, in *Amadeus* — "beloved by God!" — while Salieri himself, with all his heartfelt desire to praise God through music, is doomed to mediocrity, just like the rest of us.

Salieri's descriptive terms for the opening of Mozart's Adagio — *pulse, squeezebox, unwavering high note* — work all the more magically because the movie's soundtrack gives us the music while Salieri speaks the words. But there is more, so much more magic at work in this music, waiting to be heard, if we can learn the ingredients of its spell.

Those bassoons and basset horns, that single oboe and clarinet, are all a sign of something very specific in Mozart's music-making. In the aristocratic world of the patrons who supported Mozart's composing, music for wind instruments functioned as entertainment for out of doors. The greater capacity of wood-winds (over strings) to project their sound far and wide lends their music the freedom to be served *al fresco*. Indeed, Mozart's glorious set of Serenades and Divertimenti for Winds, including the "Gran Partita," was sometimes commissioned as the musical fare for palace garden parties. But even when the weather was unseasonable and the concert brought indoors, the performance of a wind piece diverted the company all the more with its suggestion of Mother Nature's sweet airs and wayward clemency.

When we come to hear the iconographic fitness of this Adagio music to the open air — and specifically to the garden — a whole new landscape of significance attends the music, fertilizing our simple enjoyment of it. But this *plein air* iconography goes even deeper into the cultural soil of the music (*culture* literally means "dug-up soil"), down to the dark, nocturnal, intimate function at the root of the music, erotic to the core, and so gallantly and serviceably appropriated for musical entertainment at an eighteenth-century garden party.

What is a "serenade," after all, even after Mozart has aggrandized and sophisticated it into a *Gran Partita*? It is a song of love, of unfulfilled desire, to be sung at night under the moon by the serenader to his lady, beneath her window, willing her to come down and loiter in the garden with him. It is Cyrano's vicarious song to Roxanne (alas, poor Cyrano), Romeo's to Juliet — so importunate is his that he cannot remain below, but leaps to his charge even as he launches his serenade — Ben's and Buddy's to their Phyllis and Sally in Stephen Sondheim's "Waiting For the Girls Upstairs," and, in the recent movie adaptation of *The Importance of Being Earnest*, it is Ernest's and Algie's, goofily serenading their sweethearts with "Lady Come Down." It is the misfit poet Billy Collins', fingering a nameless instrument "it took many days and nights to invent."

Proper to its *Serenade* context, the opening "pulse" of Mozart's Adagio — the rusty squeezebox — is both *parody* and *parroting* of a poor instrument in the hands of a poor lover, standing beneath the window in all his paltry inadequacy, playing his heart out to the beautiful girl above. Lo and behold! There she is, standing at the window, in all her unattainable glory, the high, unwavering oboe note that gives purpose and meaning and motive to the comical pulse below. The music shows us both the serenader and his lady; it presents to us the space between them, the remoteness of these two characters from each other, but somehow, miraculously, affirms their intimate connection. The wedding of two such disparate sonorities — the one almost ridiculous, the other sublime — is a double sign of both the distance between two potential lovers — the paltry fellow and his perfect lady — and of their potential union.

It is precisely such disparity that Salieri recognizes in the nature of Mozart himself: a sublime music bursting forth with unaccountable divinity from a ridiculous fellow. But even worse for Salieri is the recognition that his own music will be heard in the long run as the rusty squeezebox, while Mozart's singular achievement holds unwaveringly on high throughout the ages.

And it all happens — via a newly activated iconographic imagination — right out in the open, under a night sky, where wishes are tendered to the teeming stars, but only a very few granted (oh, how our own voices leap up with Jiminy Cricket's!).

On this very same ground, Mozart works out the final act of his *Marriage of Figaro*, in which the right and proper lovers are at last reconciled to each other in the only place where their darkly comical trials could be so well resolved: the precincts of a palace garden.

It is just here, in full view of Mozart's operatic stage, that another vast and generous sign is vouchsafed to us — and to *povero Salieri* — by Mozart's astonishing Adagio: the vocal impetus of *all* Mozart's music. From his prompter's pit, Mozart gives us all the right cues: the opening bassoons and basset horns signal a vamp for the entrance of the divas, who appear on high as an ensemble of *voices*, a song without words, an *aria* unscripted but as vividly dramatic as any number in Mozart's great operas. When, as Salieri exclaims, the clarinet takes over and sweetens the oboe "into a phrase of such delight," we are in the presence of the Contessa and Susanna, Anna and Elvira, Dorabella and Fiordiligi, all those pairs of Mozartian graces who meet and greet each other in contests of vocal delight. "Soave il vento," sing the two deceived sisters in Mozart's opera *Così fan tutte*, while their deceiver Don Alfonso accompanies them below, his baritone voice sounding like a rusty, philosophical squeezebox.

The correspondence of instrumental sonority and operatic sentiment invites us to go a step further in our iconographic decoding of the Adagio. It is a risky step to take because it invokes a possible biographical source for the energy of the music, and everybody knows that the inner life of art is different from the life of the artist who made it — or else we wouldn't need art, only biography. So I will venture ahead, lightly but firmly.

In "Soave il vento," the heartbroken Dorabella and Fiordiligi bid farewell to the departing ship, which bears their fiancés away to war. The two ladies wish their lovers calm winds for their voyage. *Calm winds!* The phrase may be too good to be true, but how can I ignore such a gift? The Adagio's "calm winds" (basset horns, bassoons, French horns, oboes, and clarinets) also breathe a valedictory air. In the very act of "hanging there unwavering," the single oboe note expresses a desire to stay, or to stay the departure of another. The clarinet takes over so as to prolong the farewell and delay the inevitable parting, which becomes such sweetened sorrow in the hands of this answering instrument. As the movement goes, so the sweetness darkens, collapsing into lamenting strains of minor mode. But the oboe and clarinet bravely hang on, singing their hearts out to a hope of permanency that is all the more palpable for being so fugitive.

I am not trying to *explain* why this slow movement of the "Gran Partita" is so moving. How could anyone do that? Instead, I am offering both an intimate iconographic source of its boundless sentiment and a *modus operandi* for accessing that richness. In short, I am *paying attention* to Mozart at large. I am hazarding a suggestion — one that is grounded in both stylistic evidence and interpretive chutzpah — that the composer had a dependable "iconography of valediction" to draw upon, which he deploys with equal expressiveness for a libretto that calls for it ("Soave il vento") or an instrumental work *that does not* (the Adagio of our Serenade in B-Flat). And so the feeling of the Adagio movement is a typical instance of Mozart's *supererogation*: an excessive generosity of sentiment, uncalled for, unwarranted, and therefore partaking of the quality of grace, which we earn just by being alive to the music, by paying it in its own coin of attention.

There is no reason for this Adagio from the Wind Serenade to bid farewell; "reason" does not come into it. Valediction is an unreasonable experience, as Mozart knew all too well. He bids final farewell to his mother on her deathbed in a Paris apartment, far from home and friends. He bids farewell to his father and his hometown and goes off to Vienna, just at the time when he writes this Adagio (in *Amadeus*, we see and hear him conduct the "Gran Partita" at one of his final concerts for the Archbishop of Salzburg). He bids farewell to the first great love of his life, Aloysia Weber, and settles on her little sister instead. In every one of these cases, Mozart makes the best of a bad thing, turning his sorrow into sweetness (a deeper bond with father and sister, a

larger scope for his music in a new city, a happy and companion-
able marriage). Likewise, the deceptive farewell ensemble "Soave
il vento" in *Così fan tutte* (those wicked boyfriends aren't going
away on the ship at all!) sets up the richest possible deployment of
Cupid's arrows in the quiver of Mozart's music. As for the Adagio
itself: "I don't know why you say goodbye, I say hello." This line
from a Beatles song provides the refrain of every importunate
serenader strumming his lute below a lady's window.

There is one particular farewell that Mozart's music seems to
address at length — the very first departure of all, and the conclusive one for humanity. This sweet, breeze-blown Adagio, like so
much of Mozart's music, may give us a taste of the Garden before
the Fall. The pulse beats with the pristine joy of all Creation and
the high melody between oboe and clarinet (Eve and Adam?)
sings of that Edenic pleasure, in all its short-lived glory. To a
fallen, vindictive Lucifer like Salieri, this flavor of Paradise is too
tantalizing, and thus unbearable. The effect on all Mozart lovers
is not dissimilar, even if we have less at stake than Salieri does
in the music's beauty. But do we? How are we not to believe in
Eden, when Mozart presents it to us so vividly, in such sweet and
tormenting attainability, surpassing all petty doctrinal renderings of the place?

Composers have always drawn upon audible signs as raw
material to be manipulated, combined, broken down, obliterated,
and reinvested with new meaning. I hope to instigate a dialogue
with you, dear reader, about this intimate iconography, about
its value, its limits, its impact on your experience of the music.
Music's signage — instrumental, rhythmic, melodic, harmonic,
dramatic, mimetic of things in the world, pictorial, literary,
sociological, historical, etc. — is nothing more or less than its
intrinsic stuff, its *inner life*, shaped by masters into deathless form.
Whatever the period or genre — a Classical serenade, a Romantic
symphony, a rock 'n' roll song — the composer purposefully
and expressively draws upon a vast reservoir of musical "icons."
In Mozart's Adagio, the icons are recognizable for their social

context (the "windy" garden-party entertainment), pragmatic dramaturgy (the necessity of valedictory music in his operas), or ritual function (an invocation of the archetypal lover's serenade). They are always vulnerable to the imaginative transformations he plies them with. Mozart's iconographic interplay with his various sources of musical energy generates a polyphony of signification perfectly in accord with the polyphony of instrumental voices. In Focillon's terms, Mozart's summoning of these diverse signs all at once — garden-party music, serenading music, operatic music, and farewell music — practically "breaks down" and "obliterates" those original meanings and subject matters, so that new, unanticipated meanings can attach themselves to the form of his Adagio. By willfully and ingeniously making his icons so unstable and insecure, he moves them into new regions of feeling. That's what's called *composing*. It's also a good synopsis of what happens in an opera. Perhaps that is why Mozart, whenever asked to sign his autograph, often autographed his sign: *Wolfgang Amadé Mozart, compositore delle opere.*

Much like a Yiddish idiom brought into English, we can catch the drift of audible signs without actually being able to identify them. For instance, when my father used to say to me, "Quit *hockin mir a chainik*," I knew he was telling me to stop pestering him. But when I found out years later that he was telling me to stop rattling like a noisy tea kettle, I wanted to raise him from the dead so I could hear him say it again and *know* what he really meant, so I could mindfully stand alongside him in the world of cultural signs he was generously (and with splendid irritability) bestowing upon me.

Likewise, how can you completely enjoy the interplay of musical signs if you cannot recognize them? The various, even contradictory iconographic strategies this book explores will yield a new appreciation of the enormous *intelligence* and the wide-ranging, beautifully allusive and combinatory *imagination* of composers of vastly divergent styles and technical materials. We will decode the signs composers give us in their music

— sounds that invoke very particular ideas and images and cultural contexts — and reveal the ingenuity with which certain great works deploy recognizable, conventional, and infinitely variable figures in a musical landscape. None of this can be done systematically. Each piece of music reinvents "the code" and demands a unique set of approaches. In reading Sherlock Holmes stories, I am struck by Conan Doyle's trick of showing us that it is usually the clue Holmes finds most obvious that feels most mystifying to the reader (and to poor Watson). So, too, in studying music, where the "Duh!" signs are often just as inscrutable as the "Huh?" signs. As your guide, I promise to stay closer in spirit to Watson than to Holmes, and do my best to take nothing for granted in our musical investigations.

Any iconography of music will work only if it can be understood as the respiring, perspiring, aspiring, inspiring — at times despairing, at others repairing — inner life of music. We must find a way *to move through our knowledge of signs* to some deeper relationship with our music — and our paintings, and our poems, and the spaces we inhabit — some synthesis of innocence and experience, some point where we become ready for anything, completely alive to the surprise of form, to the unexpected shapes art takes and how they affect us — signs, wonders, and all.

The subtitle of this book is *Essays from a Musical Ground*. Music has always served as the basis, the bass line, the *baseline*, from which I have pitched my imagination over the net dividing the arts from one another. In this book, I risk commenting upon Caravaggio, Rembrandt, and a handful of poets. What do I know about art or poetry? Only enough to say *this* to you, dear reader: it is not important to be an expert, only to be a lover. Expertise is the one thing we do not need in this life. Look where the experts have got us. All we need is love. "Knowledge is the harvest of attentions." This is something Guy Davenport wrote, and I will always love him for delivering this simple, cultivable truth.

My two-year-old boy sings "Twinkle, twinkle, little star" straight through, his performance a marvel of toddling intonation conned from Telly the Monster on *Sesame Street*. Following Telly's lead, he pauses for breath and launches into "A-B-C-D-E-F-G" on the same tune. A pause. Then, "Baa baa black sheep, have you any wool," same key, same tune, same astonishing recognition of patterns belonging to this fleeting moment in a child's life. Like Dorothy's, like Jiminy's, like Bloody Mary's, Izzy's voice leaps up to the star, but then to the flowing, following letters of the alphabet, and then to the black sheep. There can be no question of "word painting" when the same tune applies to three utterly disparate lyrics. Still, the shape of the tune (and it is Mozart's tune too, in his set of piano variations *Ah, vous dirai je, Maman*, K. 265) is a sign . . . of what, I wonder. How I wonder what you are, you unreachable sign. Izzy knows. It is a diamond in his sky. But he won't tell.

Chapter 2

The Redress of Music

you that were
formed to begin with
you that were cried out
you that were spoken
to begin with
to say what could not be said

ancient precious
and helpless ones

say it

(from "To The Words," by W. S. Merwin,
mid-September, 2001)

I. THE OFFENSE OF ART

It is September 11, 2001. When I awoke this morning, I knew without thinking I had to greet the cool, brilliant, early autumn day at close quarters. As I was driving the five miles to Warner Woods, where I would walk along one of my favorite trails up to the highest and most panoramic hilltop in the park, the first plane crashed into the World Trade Center. I didn't know this at the time, for in the car I was listening to a tape of a magnificent choral work by Ralph Vaughan Williams, his *Dona Nobis Pacem*. I'd heard this music many times in the past few weeks, over and over again in the car. This time, I reckon, I laid myself open to it, for as the chorus and orchestra took up Walt Whitman's words — his "word over all" that will make "war and all its deeds of carnage utterly lost," that will "wash again and ever again this soiled world" — I found myself weeping at the impossibility of this vision, and at my own folly for holding fast to it, for grasping unreasonably its rightness, even though it would never come. It was at that very minute, as I now calculate, that the first aircraft tore into the side of the tower, killing hundreds in an instant, dooming thousands of others.

After my walk in the woods, I drove home and went to work in my study. I had already traveled deep into that familiar, feverish territory I enter whenever I get a good start in my composing day, when I looked up from my manuscript page and out the window, and saw a car I didn't recognize in our driveway. I got up from the piano to investigate. Just then, the phone rang. It was my wife's friend, calling from her car in our driveway, making sure it was all right to stop in. My wife and I went to greet her at the front door and she asked if we had heard the news. I turned on the television and learned of all the hijackings, the death and destruction.

It would be wrong to say that I was surprised. My earlier sobbing spell has much to do with this, I think. Perhaps my fit of recognition on the way to the park, brought on by that terrible, beautiful music in the car, somehow prepared me for the insupportable shock of these events.

The Red Cross rejected my blood last year because of mad cow disease restrictions (I spend time every year in England), so now I called their office to make a cash donation instead. Just as I hung up, my mother rang us from Philadelphia to assure us that my nephew Zachary had been safely evacuated from Stuyvesant High School, located one block from the World Trade Center, and site of a bomb threat on top of everything else. With the first phone call, I reached out a feeble hand to the collapsed tents of others; through the second, I ascertained that my own family tent was secure.

Beyond these miserable gestures, I am powerless to do anything. The notion of carrying on my composing today runs through my head like a ghoulish joke. Having abandoned one keyboard, I turn to the other, truly not knowing what I am doing, unsure of how susceptible I am to charges of insensitivity or indiscretion for bringing up music or movies at such a time. I am past caring about that.

The early stages of shock do not allow for much grieving. But a memorial to the dead and to the survivors, and to those shoved violently into the nightmare of sudden loss, can be worked on, must be raised, one piece at a time, starting today, now, when there is nothing else to do, constructed painstakingly in the ghastly void where those unconscionably vulnerable twin towers once stood.

The pleasures of music — and of art generally — must, one way or another, always be reckoned an *offense* against the relentless presence of cruelty, disaster and loss in the world. A song goes up, and flies always in the face of all the destruction and abuse of life going on at every moment of history. The ambiguity of the word "offense" is intentional. Our task is to uncover the difference between *the one way and the other*: between art that is *offensive* in the light of suffering, and art that is vigilantly, brightly on the *offense* against that dismal light. *L'havdil!* This is the insistent task given to the student by the rabbi throughout the Talmud: *distinguish!* Draw a line between one kind of act and another, between the sacred and the profane, between what is specially worthy of your attention and what is merely worthy (for everything under the sun is worthy of your attention), and you will become smart. More than that, you will be imitating God, who in the first place distinguished light from darkness, day from night, the waters above from the waters below, *kosher* from *trayf*.

I invoke this Talmudic analogy as a way of introducing the operative principle at work (*l'havdil!*) in my own *offensive* against what is *offensive in art*. Jews have no monopoly on either wisdom or suffering. What we do have is an ongoing chutzpah to try to use the first to understand the second — with little success, but stubborn persistence. Our book of Job famously acknowledges the impossibility of art — in Job's case, the persistent praise of God — either to forestall or redress human catastrophe. That's what makes it a great work of art.

Steven Spielberg could have usefully pondered this paradox. The following critique of his celebrated film has two purposes. It is meant to invite those who have seen it to go back and look again, and to encourage first-time viewers to go straight to it and make up their own minds. Please bear in mind that my commentary is a reflection of both awe and desperation over the film — awe because of its haunting images and emotional virtuosity, and desperation on account of how much I wanted to admire it, and was not able to.

Some of the points I make were also made by reviewers when the movie first came out in 1993, but I adapt them here, along with my own ideas, in order to aid and abet my main objective: to give a vivid example of how art — and more particularly music — can take an offensive (i.e., objectionable) turn when it falls under the shadow of disaster.

Schindler's List is a seriously flawed film, for the same reason that the art of music is flawed, right down to the ground: it dares to make bearable that which cannot ever be borne.

The sentimentality of Spielberg's *Schindler* marks the perfect climax of his happy career. Every emotion he gives to us in the film, like every emotion he has always given us, is both authentic — by virtue of its visual power — and unearned, apart from the cash we lay down at the ticket window (this "ode on egregiously unearned" music will be a theme of the next chapter). Spielberg shows us just enough to make us feel wholeheartedly, and this is fine when sharks and extra-terrestrials are at stake. But it will not do once he has made the exponential leap to an emotional arena where the only way to feel anything real is for the heart to be shattered.

The emotional force of the final scenes of *Schindler's List* hinges on our grasp of the hero's moral development. We come to love this man Schindler, the Jew-saver, with all his flaws, as he takes possession of his own goodness. Our love gives us insight into the pain he feels, and thus we are able to take the pain upon ourselves. His grief at not saving more Jewish lives during the Nazi Holocaust becomes our grief; our tears are given a localized destination, an outlet, a way home to the heart.

But the real *pleasure* we take from observing and identifying with the growth of Schindler's character over the course of the movie is a *distraction* from the task of monstrous recognition laid on us by the film's historical subject. We accept this reprieve from history with both unconscious and reciprocally affirming gratitude. In the fulfillment of this exchange between director and viewer, pleasure shrinks into diversion, and from diversion into falsehood. (These terms will be treated further in the next chapter.)

In real life, Spielberg has been a tireless champion of historical accuracy, a great deal of his energy and income since *Schindler* pouring into his worldwide Holocaust Oral History Project. But in his film, where he has by far the most impact on our culture, Spielberg opens the door onto the tiger of implacable fact and reveals to us instead a sweet lady of sorrow, clad in dulcet violin tones and leading us by the arm towards that magical intersection where fact and artful narrative are indistinguishable. In the closing scene, the actors walk arm in arm with their real-life counterparts to lay a stone on the Oskar Schindler memorial. Spielberg obliterates the all-important line between history and storytelling with this final, unforgettable, and unforgivable image.

Like some unwitting Nero, Itzhak Perlman plays his fiddle on the soundtrack *while children burn*. This distressing but precisely accurate image takes its cue from a well-known and horrific dictum of Irving Greenberg, the director of the United States Holocaust Memorial Museum: "Do not say anything about the Holocaust that you could not say in the presence of burning children." The violin cleanses us of the unbearable stench that covers us whenever we go into that vortex of cruelty called the *Shoah*. Perlman's playing is offensive to the exact degree that it is musically affecting.

Ah, how the violin melody greases the wheel of our mourning. Whoever does not cry at such a cathartic pass is a monster indeed. But I tell you, out of the shallows of my own paltry woe, it sometimes takes a monster to face a monster (what Nietzsche famously warned against, I am insisting upon). Here, the *dæmonic* as a radical principle of artistic truth-telling rears its head. We must become dæmons in order to wage war against dæmons. The peculiar presence of the diphthong in my spelling of the word pays tribute to Thomas Mann's definitive celebration of the dæmonic as a necessary element of music, in his novel, *Doktor Faustus* (see Chapter 5). Meanwhile, in John Williams' Hollywood recording studio, dæmons need not apply.

For all these sins of misdirection, Spielberg atones with one matchless moment of filmic horror. The Nazis are clearing the ghetto, rooting out all the Jews hiding in attics and under floorboards. In the midst of the mayhem, one of the guards takes a break from his murderous work when he arrives at a Jewish apartment with a piano. He sits down and plays a classical piece by heart, and he plays with talent and gusto. Though I have seen the movie several times, and have recognized the piece immediately each time, I always determinedly block out its identity afterward (of ironic help is the fact that a couple of other guards in the scene argue about what their mate is playing). Here is a moment of crashing insight about the helplessness of beauty to make any difference in the world. It is a fantasy to think that Bach (oh, hell, it *was* Bach, wasn't it?) might turn the hand of this SS guard away from its evil work because that hand was transformed by the configuration of keys it has just played. The presence of music at such an appalling event is not only incongruous, it is *offensive*, and Spielberg thrusts this irony in our faces with fearless intelligence. Right *there*, at the destruction of the ghetto, where it counts, Spielberg grasps clearly, searingly, the nausea that attends music of the most sublime beauty under those circumstances. And so I am at a loss to understand how he could have given such a free hand throughout the movie to composer John Williams, the sentimental pleasures of whose score shrink into unconscionable diversions, and thence precipitously into falsehoods.

The soundtrack to *Superman* is a masterpiece, perhaps the finest film score of the past forty years. Here, there is a perfect match between the comic-book fantasy of Clark Kent's secretive and redemptive greatness (a humanity-saving Oskar Schindler from planet Krypton) and John Williams' secretive and plagiarizing redemption of nearly every great composer of the modern classical repertoire. Williams should stick to comic books. His wonderfully Wagnerian music to the *Star Wars* Trilogy unintentionally fulfills, in a more accessible medium, the half-baked, sophomoric mythopoeia of Wagner's operas (evil Semites and all). Meanwhile, Schindler's list is no comic book. Just listen to a single movement from one of the string quartets composed by Viktor Ullmann — killed at Auschwitz in 1944 — and the obscenity of Itzhak Perlman's violin playing in *Schindler's List* becomes clear. This is why I felt compelled to quote Williams'

Schindler theme in my own *Songs of Rest and Unrest*. It was an ordeal — both welcome and necessary in my spiritual life — to try to turn its obscene beauty into something more seemly, something grounded in the vastness of what Schindler could not rescue.

The pleasures of a piece of music can, in the best hands, sometimes be reckoned an attack, a reproach, an *offensive* against the relentless presence of cruelty, disaster, and loss in the world. A song goes up, flies in the face of despair, and calls pain and destructiveness to hard account for their crimes. A very few musical works achieve this miracle of redress on a grand scale, with comprehensive courage, swimming forcefully against the evil tides of history, enlisting faith, philosophy, and poetry as their allies. Bach's *St. Matthew Passion*, Mahler's *"Resurrection" Symphony* and Vaughan Williams' *Dona Nobis Pacem* are monumental examples, each one arising from a divergent and idiosyncratic theological position. I owe the title of this chapter to the poet Seamus Heaney, who defines "The Redress of Poetry" in the following terms at the very end of his eponymous essay:

> . . . it is when the spirit is called extravagantly beyond the course that the usual life plots for it, when outcry or rhapsody is wrung from its own solitude and distinctness . . .

Much great music delivers this shattering and self-estranging summons to us, demanding that we depart from our usual course and submit to the famous imperative of Rilke's archaic torso of Apollo: *you must change your life.*

But there is yet another mode of redress that works on more familiar ground, where composers attach themselves deliberately to the everyday sphere. When pieces of music focus purposefully on the sublunary world of human striving, they embrace a spiritual principle that *less is much more*. What else can our songs really know but what we see and hear and feel every day, on the hither side of transcendence, in the world where we grow to love earthly things, where we evolve through these acts of loving? These works, in close allegiance to human suffering, underscore the drama of *this* quotidian life, and a large measure of their triumph is that they help us feel that we belong here too, since everything we hope for can be found here, not above some "starry canopy" (Schiller's doubtful phrase in the "Ode to Joy," so pregnant with skepticism). If history gives us a chance, if horror recedes long enough for us to proceed with our lives and realize the blessing of life itself, then we can go about our serious business of loving and working, of making and redressing mistakes in love and work. Shakespeare, the Beatles, and Beethoven show the way.

II. A THREE-WAY TIE: SHAKESPEARE, THE BEATLES, AND BEETHOVEN

Music to hear, why hear'st thou music sadly?
Sweets with sweets war not, joy delights in joy:
Why lov'st thou that which thou receiv'st not gladly,
Or else receiv'st with pleasure thine annoy?
If the true concord of well-tunèd sounds,
By unions married, do offend thine ear,
They do but sweetly chide thee, who confounds
In singleness the parts that thou shouldst bear.
Mark how one string, sweet husband to another,
Strikes each in each by mutual ordering;
Resembling sire and child and happy mother,
Who, all in one, one pleasing note do sing:
Whose speechless song, being many, seeming one,
Sings this to thee, "Thou single wilt prove none."

(Shakespeare, Sonnet VIII)

Hey Jude, don't make it bad.
Take a sad song and make it better.
Remember to let her into your heart,
Then you can start to make it better.

And anytime you feel the pain, hey Jude, refrain,
Don't carry the world upon your shoulder . . .
Nanana na na nanana na . . .

. . . And don't you know that it's just you, hey Jude, you'll do,
The movement you need is on your shoulder.
Nanana na na nanana na . . .

. . . Remember to let her under your skin,
Then you'll begin to make it
Better better better better better better, oh.

Na na na nanana na, nanana na, hey Jude . . .

(Paul McCartney, "Hey Jude")

Shakespeare's assignment from his patron for Sonnet VIII was uncomplicated: to persuade a young nobleman to abandon his sad and single state, get married, and get children. It is typical of the bard that he fashioned something more lovely for the wayward boy than a motivational lecture on primogeniture.

Paul McCartney's "assignment" was more poignant, less formal, and something that actually preceded the composition of "Hey Jude": he wanted to cheer up Julian Lennon, a little boy whose folks John and Cynthia were splitting up. Leave it to Paul to turn a cross-town pep talk to a boy about his divorcing parents into a song that takes on a world of possible love-sorrowings ("Hey, Julian, don't make it bad, hey Jules, hey Jude . . .").

"Mark how one string, sweet husband to another, / Strikes each in each by mutual ordering," Sonnet VIII entreats. Lyrical poetry has always understood the wedding of musical sounds to be the finest analogy we have for the weaving together of two loving souls. In this poem, Shakespeare broadens the loom to include offspring. The different notes of a lute song resemble "sire and child and happy mother, / Who, all in one, one pleasing note do sing." This "true concord of well-tunèd sounds" not only provides an ideal image of oneness for man, woman, and child; it also serves as an attack against singleness, a *reproach* against withholding oneself from love and marital union. The music "offends the ear" of the introverted prince because music itself, by the very nature of its harmonious dispositions, is an *offense* against loneliness and withdrawal.

Shakespeare concludes his chiding of the solitary youth (his Jude) by giving actual voice to the strings of the lute. The music speaks the chill warning, "Thou single wilt prove none." Mark how the poem's arithmetic has a marvelous consistency, tending always towards economy: that which is manifold (musical notes, families) is one; that which is merely one (the sad, lonely, retreating boy) will prove to be none.

In finally giving speech to "speechless song," Shakespeare seems to affirm his own poetic art. Words themselves are given the last word, even if they are only words the poet imagines a lute *might* sing, if it had a tongue. Language beats all — especially music, which can only go as far as being an *audible sign* for the urgent idea which it is the poet's task to translate into grammatical speech.

In "Hey Jude," however, Paul McCartney and his fellow Beatles end up favoring "speechless song" over words. As the verses and bridges of the song unfold, the language of encouragement and consolation becomes more and more fitful, less and less coherent (though certainly more powerful in the process). After coaxing Jude through various feelings in the first two verses, Paul tries the new strategy of appealing to his reason in the first bridge: "For well you know that it's a fool who plays it cool by making his world a little colder." Apparently, these blandishments do not work either, and the first burst of "na na na"s which end the bridge indicates Paul's growing frustration with the bounds of reasonable discourse.

In the following verse, the urgency of Paul's message brings about the first, provisional collapse of the lordship of words. While Paul is busy telling Jude, "You have found her, now go and get her," we hear *another* Paul at the same time, enjoining Jude to "let it out and let it in." But *this* line of words and music belongs properly to the next section of the song. Oops! He prematurely expostulated! By anticipating the song's later lyrics now — singing uncannily against himself in jarring, not-exactly-harmonious counterpoint — Paul shows us language tumbling on top of language, asserting itself in unseemly haste, resorting to desperate measures, undoing its own linear syntax, all because it is always insufficient to the emotional task at hand. Paul speaks in tongues, and his ecstasy takes us one step further towards the grace that lies beyond words.

When Paul McCartney came up with the words "the movement you need is on your shoulder" (in the second bridge), he thought he would delete them from the final version. But John Lennon loved the line. Paul remembers their conversation: "I'm saying, 'It's crazy, it doesn't make any sense at all.'" To which John replied, "Sure it does, it's great," and convinced him to keep it in the song.

One *could* make a rational case that in the first bridge, he tells Jude, "Don't carry the world upon your shoulder," so it feels right to hear the word "shoulder" again in the second bridge; and it furthermore makes sense that the reappearance of "shoulder" reinforces the song's recurrent idea that all Jude needs is already within his own body, rather than something he has to take upon himself from the world outside.

But Paul was right about what he'd done: the line itself, *the movement you need is on your shoulder*, is nonsense ("a tidy compendium of pop clichés," Tim Riley calls it). Words tend invariably towards disarray, and the magnificence of this particular lyric lies in its cheerful embrace of that chaos. We go with Paul through the dark glass of that senseless line, and there, on the other side, we find him again and he gives us the movement we need, on our shoulder, in our throat, down where the lung meets the diaphragm ("so let it out and let it in"); and as the bridge goes into the final verse, he marks for us once more how the syllables strike each in each by mutual ordering: Na na na *na* na *na* na na *na*: Jude, Paul, all of us: we need to move into "speechless song."

In Sonnet VIII, Shakespeare wants to turn his speechless lute into a singing voice. In "Hey Jude," Paul McCartney wants to turn his singing voice into a speechless lute (or electric guitar), the limit of whose articulateness is something approaching the sound "na."

This shift from words to "na"s at the end of each bridge foreshadows the larger movement of the song towards its vast coda of "na"s. But before the song's farewell to language, Paul makes time for one last verse, one more go at words, a last-ditch effort to say what *can* be said. In this last verse, Paul gives up on finding new, right words that might heal poor Jude and bring him back into the human fold. Instead, he enlists his friends John and George to help him out as he doubles back on the lyrics of the first verse, whose simplicity and directness are unsurpassed ("take a sad song and make it better").

John and Paul and George have never sounded sweeter together, more natural, more attuned to each other's voices, than they do in this verse. They are clearly having the time of their lives, and if this demonstration of how much joy attends the company of loved ones cannot shake Jude out of his blues, nothing will. One glorious sigh, "Oh!" comes from one of them (which? who?) after the line, "Remember to let her under your skin," and it's a promise of such fulfillment, such comprehensive bliss, that the one who sighs cannot go on, but mutters some uncatchable words instead.

The presence of this unsung muttering sets the seal on the limits of words as a vehicle for the song's emotions. The spoken line sounds like some sort of direction by one of the band to his fellows. According to reliable witnesses, it's actually Paul cursing over a wrong note he hit by mistake (he's only human, like the rest of us, which is the point he's trying to make to Jude). In any case, when it comes, it feels something like "Hold on, boys, here we go!" just before they take flight, up along a blue-note-laden arpeggio on the verse's final word "better," into the higher, better atmosphere of speechless song which is the four-minute-long coda (longer than the whole verbal structure that precedes it).

Those muttered words of Paul just before the coda are, to my bewildered and grateful mind, the closest equivalent we have in modern song to the inscrutable word *Selah* of the Psalms. From its textual context, various translators have determined that *Selah* could be an more emphatic version of the punctuating and affirming word *Amen*; alternatively, it may possibly have functioned as a musical direction to the original vocal performers of the psalms to shift from one mode to another; finally, it might have served as a technical instruction to the resident orchestra of the Temple in Jerusalem to play an instrumental (wordless!) interlude. Whichever option you like best, *Selah* means, "Hold on, boys, here we go!"

The near-wordless coda surpasses cajolery, exceeds consolation, and surrenders to music's native joy. There is something almost tyrannical here in the way Jude's private pain is overtaken by Paul's vocal abandon, the Beatles' accompanying celebration, and the instruments' all-encompassing ground bass. By this time, Jude will have heeded the call and hitched his soul to the Beatles — whose only true word among all the "na"s is his name — or else "must creep tearfully away from our circle" (a dark line from Schiller's "Ode to Joy"). Like Beethoven, the Beatles allow for *no vacancy at the holiday in music*, which they set before us in the coda of "Hey Jude" (more on the word *holiday* in Chapter 3). You're either in, or you're in. There is no out. "Creeping tearfully away" just does not seem an option, when the entire universe has become a festival, when one by one, verse by verse, voice by voice, instrument by instrument, the Beatles (and, as we shall see, Beethoven) build up an additive structure of harmonious joy that sweeps aside all resistance and makes unthinkable the exclusion of even one single person (the very "Jude" both Shakespeare and Paul are singing to).

Schiller's Ode echoes the sentiments of Sonnet VIII:

> *Whoever has created*
> *An abiding friendship,*
> *Or has won*
> *A true and loving wife,*
> *All who can call at least one soul theirs,*
> *Join in our song of praise.*

Both poets tell you that "Thou single wilt prove none." Schiller then deepens the chill of this warning with the two lines I've already quoted: *But any who cannot [call at least one soul theirs] must creep tearfully away from our circle.* There seems to be a discrepancy between these cruel and banishing words of Schiller's Ode (however fleeting they are in the overall poem, they are crucial to the poem's spirit) and the unadulterated generosity of Beethoven's musical setting of the poem in his Ninth Symphony. I have been fishing for clues about the relationship between words and music in Sonnet VIII and "Hey Jude." Now I will cast the net further, to catch Beethoven's Ninth if I can.

Beethoven labored for many years over his decision to use Schiller's Ode in the grand choral finale of the *Ninth*. But once decided, he was characteristically adamant about the necessity of words. The last movement of the symphony dramatizes the insufficiency of instrumental music without words. Wordless cellos and basses "sing" ("bark" would be a more apt expression), in a brutal mock-up of an opera *recitativo*. They call to account each of the three previous movements of the symphony (a fragment of each is played), and each is found wanting (more on this scenario in the next chapter).

In the Ninth, then, Beethoven seems to uphold Shakespeare's lording of words over music: the finale suggests that instrumental music alone is incapable of articulating true joy. Poetry can do it, though. Eventually, the "shadow-voices" of the cellos/basses are replaced by an actual baritone voice, and the instrumental variations of the melody of joy are replaced by solo and choral versions of the tune.

A good measure of "what makes Shakespeare and Beethoven great" (a line from Meredith Willson's *The Music Man*) is the vexing fact that any effort to hold either of them to something like a concrete belief, or to know exactly where they stand on a particular aesthetic question, is doomed to failure. This is why I have always added the word "seems" wherever I have tried to make any claims about their rhetorical purposes, which — *being many, seeming one* — are impossible to pin down. Their "philosophies" are as protean as their strategies for creating new forms. Any single truth-claim about Shakespeare or Beethoven "will prove none."

In the end, Shakespeare's sonnet leaves the question of the relative power of words and music generously open to irony. Shakespeare, after all, is the one who must provide the words for the speechless song of the lute, which surely does not need them. Likewise, the choral finale of the *Ninth* sustains a possible, ironic tension between Beethoven's love for Schiller's poem and his ultimate contempt for it. His setting passes quickly through the "creep tearfully away" bit of Schiller's poem as if he were embarrassed by the text. With a much blither spirit, however, Beethoven seizes upon another line of Schiller's and simply will not let it go: "All people become brothers" (*Alle Menschen werden Brüder*). By the symphony's end, we hear this line so many times that we might just scream at one more mention of "Menschen." Schiller's "Kiss for all the World" is given comparable emphasis. The music distills the poem down to several essential lines; in the process, the integrity of Schiller's text is both torn asunder and redefined. Beethoven shows us that the notion of music's being incapable of articulating true joy without words entirely misses the point, which is that *words and music need each other, just as people do* (Jude knows this now, we hope).

In all four of these works — Shakespeare's, Schiller's, Beethoven's, and the Beatles' — the spirit that drives the beating heart of the poem or song is *generosity*. Even Schiller's nasty exclusion of the schlemiel who has no wife or friends is meant to rid the company of an ungenerous intruder. All four artists are generous in their art; at the same time, they are devoted to the idea of generosity *itself*. In the greatness and goodness of all these works, a private realm of woe is overtaken and overturned by the clamorous call of public joy. Would it not behoove us to imagine what such a song would sound like now, and how we might earn it?

Chapter 3

Earning Your Song

Hearts are not had as gifts but hearts are earned
By those that are not entirely beautiful.

(William Butler Yeats,
misquoted by Robert Pogue Harrison)

I. POSTSCRIPT ON "HEY JUDE" AND THE NINTH

"Hey, Judie, Judie, Judie, Judie, Judie!" Who *is* that so ecstatically hailing poor Jude in the coda of the song? Well, we know it's Paul doing the yelling, literally tearing up his larynx (it took him weeks to recover his voice after the recording session), while his pals hold fast to the repeated "na na na"s. But it's like no Paul we've heard before, not in this song, nor in any other. To say that the *color* of McCartney's voice has changed is to commit a very precise *double entendre*. The singer of the foregoing verses of "Hey Jude" sounds like a white man from Liverpool. The singer of these joyful shouts in the song's coda sounds like a black man from the streets of Harlem or Augusta, Georgia (the hometown of the great soul man, James Brown).

This dramatic change in the quality of Paul's voice is an audible sign of a change experienced in the character of the *persona* singing the song. The singer evolves *through the act of singing the song.* He tenders certain truths to Jude, and in the process of delivering them, he finds that these truths have consequences for himself, if he genuinely grasps and acts upon them. As always when it comes to the Beatles, critic Tim Riley sums up Paul's spiritual evolution in "Hey Jude" better than anyone:

> If the song is about self-worth and self-consolation in the face of hardship, the vocal performance itself conveys much of the journey. [Paul] begins by singing to comfort someone else, finds himself weighing his own feelings in the process, and finally, in the repeated refrains that nurture his own approbation, he comes to believe in himself.
>
> (*Tell Me Why*, p. 255)

Such spiritual transformations through dramatic song are an ancient project. Aristotle has a name for the phenomenon in his *Poetics*: *catharsis*, which means "cleansing," or "purgation." In the philosopher's account, the viewer of a drama undergoes a cathartic process through encountering the suffering of the tragic protagonist. The effect is an aesthetic one — for some Aristotle scholars, even a therapeutic one: imaginative acts of empathy depend, without irony, on the distance between the audience's position and the ordeals of the characters on stage. A proper balance of terror and pity — feelings that always threaten to overwhelm us, as they do the actors in the drama — is restored through the tragic art of the dramatic poet. For Aristotle, therefore, the most important virtue of tragedy is its *moderating* effect on the listener.

This is a far cry from Beethoven and the Beatles, who permit no such Aristotelian distance. Their music directly and

immediately constitutes an experience of suffering, an ordeal
of abiding through hardship, a reaching for truth, an upholding of goodness, an achieving of wisdom. As listeners, we bear
witness to these acts of courage and, if brave enough, we learn
what it means to hope for as much in our own travails. Ludwig
and the Fab Four do not instruct us in the art of moderating our
emotions as Sophocles and Aeschylus did, by offering a negative
example such as the fatally immoderate Oedipus or Elektra.
Rather, Beethoven and the Beatles stand as emotional role models in their own right, presenting the tremendous paradox of a
human being ascending into expressive immoderacy by way of
the most fiercely controlled and artful singing.

I keep coming back to "Hey Jude" and Beethoven's Ninth
— making a habit of them, alighting again and again on their
spreading branches — because they are, in their respective
idioms, supreme instances of a singer earning the right to sing
by doing the work of singing. Consider again the beginning of
the Ninth's finale: the strange roll call of previous movements,
brought to muster by the barking *recitativo* of cellos and basses.
All that foregoing labor — three-quarters of an hour of strenu-
ous music, Allegro, Scherzo, and Adagio — is now weighed in
the balance, and found wanting. Three movements' worth of
instrumental "singing" is summarily dismissed as insufficient to
the work at hand: the work of breaking through to joy.

Unsuccessful (to himself, at least) as a stage dramatist,
Beethoven makes his instrumental music into compensatory acts
of dramatic immediacy (and immoderacy). He would be dissatis-
fied merely showing us an Orestes suffering at the hands of fate.
Instead, as the final movement of the Ninth Symphony unfolds,
Beethoven strives to *become* Orestes, arrive at Athens, confront
the Furies, force their hand, shout them down, risk death, fulfill
his ruinous destiny, and, in the process, discover something
exceeding that tragic boundary. We watch and listen, breathless
at the magnitude of the composer's ordeal, the implacability of
his predicament, so broadly misinterpreted for musical weal

or scandalous woe by generations of listeners, from Brahms to Mahler to Sibelius to Anthony Burgess to Susan McClary to me. Beethoven is not to be scorned or pitied, as Orestes is. He is to be *emulated* (the gods forbid that we would ever emulate Orestes!). As we watch more closely and listen yet more deeply to the Ninth's finale, the wind of his ferocious joy blows through us and we learn what it means to have fortitude to this degree. At the moment in Schiller's Ode when humanity stands before God, a shudder passes through the chorus and orchestra, a passage of sheer harmonic terror, a stunned apprehension of divine regard. *This* is what it takes to achieve joy, Beethoven asserts. It's no picnic. Nor is it anything that could remotely be called happiness. It is an *ascent*, ardor-laden and exhausting. Even as the voices and instruments rise to the limit of their playable ranges, the tortuous changing of chords moves in the opposite direction, downwards, into nether regions of tonal relation. Those theorists are too parochial who insist that the progress of music can have no spatial direction, being merely sound. The God-driven crisis of the Ninth's finale proves that music exists in space, where it can go up or down — or, in this case, stretch in both directions at once, approaching the limits of its harmonic coherence.

At stake in the Ninth Symphony is nothing less than the health and integrity of Beethoven's soul. He bursts from a nearly decade-long silence in order to make this spiritual reckoning in the Ninth. The piece arises, a long-baked bread of affliction, from the blank suffering of that period (there is evidence aplenty for this interim darkness). The joyous sounds of the Ninth — like Van Gogh's towering cypresses or Dickinson's disconcerting lines of verse — must not be permitted to justify the artist's suffering, which helped to bring the art into being. Suffering simply exists; there is no justification for it. What art can do is to find a voice opposed to suffering, to fight back, to *work hard* against suffering in the only way humans know how, which is to sing, to sing our hearts out, to sing until we die.

"Hey Jude" is every bit as much of an arduous ascent as the

Ninth, all the more so on account of its compact brevity on a classical scale/inordinate length in rock 'n' roll terms. In two waves, first in the verses and then in the coda, the music comes into being like aural masonry, stone placed lovingly on stone, an additive principle of sound construction, of *sound* construction. At the start, there is only Paul's voice and a guitar. One by one, verse by verse, instruments and voices join in, tambourine, drums, electric bass, piano, the chorus of Beatles in that gorgeous vocal harmony of the final verse. The generosity of Paul's message to Jude has its exact audible counterpart in the *largesse* of the evolving ensemble of the song. By the time the brass choir enters in the coda, any possibility of the new timbre's surprise is outdone by its logical inevitability. Like the voice's pigment-shifting persona, the vast ensemble of "Hey Jude"'s coda forms a hue and cry against suffering, made out of every hue and every cry.

Rock 'n' roll, like all song since the beginning of the world, mostly sings in the color blue. *She left me, he's no good to me, she's got a ticket to ride, oh, they're writing songs of love but not for me.* Consider just how rare it is for a pop song to hold out a helping hand to another human being instead of kvetching about one. Here is a game I play with my students: name me one song, just one, that has a heart larger than its own need, a voice concerned with something other than its own misery or burning desire. In the Beatles canon, there are precisely three I can name: "She Loves You," "Dear Prudence," and "Hey Jude." Every other song grasps at love, barks at it like a dog, *oh, it's been a hard day's night, oh, I want you so bad, it's driving me mad.* Every other song holds on like a drowning man to whatever scraps of love it can get (*If I fell in love with you would you promise to be true*), begs for more scraps (*love me do, please please me*) or moans about the scraps that are gone with *yesterday*'s rubbish. And so these three exceptional songs feel like miraculous little islands of compassion in an ocean of self-absorption. "She Loves You" and "Dear Prudence" call for extensive investigation: every note of these two songs adds up to the same self-transcending generosity as "Hey Jude."

Why does rock 'n' roll, or country music, or just about any genre of popular music, so rarely cultivate explicit compassion for another person's suffering? Instead, the generosity of popular music, such as it is, remains stubbornly and prudently *subjective*: we are moved by the singer's suffering-in-love because we recognize it as our own. We identify with the music's power to the degree that it identifies our own powerlessness in the clutches of cruel Aphrodite. We look into a great love song as we look into a mirror, and for once, we can be happy in the act of recognizing our flaws, for the song makes them beautiful. This intimate, one-on-one relationship between song and listener makes rock 'n' roll the perfect vehicle for listening in a car. What else do you need when you've got a tank full of gas and a song full of spleen? Not one blessed thing, nor anybody else.

But then there's "Hey Jude," which makes an audible reality out of the illusion that every single one of God's creatures ought to be singing this song, not in a car, but in the actual world, together, a chorus of Judes, all singing through the pain, not "waiting for someone to perform with," but cutting loose because everyone can sing this one, everyone has the right to perform it, sing it down into the ground and up into the cosmos. Paul performed the song several years ago during his halftime show at the Super Bowl. Considering both the hundred thousand fans in the stadium and the billion or so television viewers, the universalizing tendency of the song's structure became a literal fact. At one point towards the end of the performance, Paul stopped singing, leaned towards the crowd, and cupped his hand to his ears, summoning the "na na na"s from untold masses like a goddamn angel, or demon, or demigod. What could a lover of "Hey Jude" and a believer in its message do, but weep for joy at such a fulfillment of the song's artistic vision?

To conclude this postscript on Beethoven and the Beatles, let's get back to where we once belonged, at the point where Paul yells "Judie, Judie, Judie, Judie" like a black man. What am I really proposing by making such an ethnically deterministic

statement? Does the audible sign of Paul's change of vocal identity in the coda of "Hey Jude" have any business being so racially
particular? Paul Robeson, Joe Williams, William Warfield, and
Bobby Short are all black men, all glorious singers; but none of
them sounds like *this*.

It's a question of musical roots. When Paul breaks out into
those shattering shouts, he approaches very close to the vocal
magic of Chuck Berry, or Little Richard, or (closest of all) James
Brown. These are the men who rocked his world at the start of
his journey, turning his little Liverpudlian music puddle into
a sea of possible musical relations. The sound of a great, wailing African-American rhythm 'n' blues voice came to express
something very specific to both Paul and John throughout their
Beatles oeuvre. Think of all those larynx-ripping moments: John
pleading "C'mon, c'mon, c'mon, c'mon baby now, twist a little
closer now" (he even adds an extra "c'mon" to the original Isley
Brothers version). Paul cutting loose, after verses full of wild
explication, with the punch line, "Got to get you into my life!"
A more restrained, but no less intense John, summoning an
inexorable ghost from the ghetto, insistently declaiming, "Come
together, right now, over me." Or Paul again, this time projecting
a black hole of misery in "I'm Down."

The voice turns black to the same degree that it turns inward.
Intuitively, and for good reason, the Beatles tapped into a certain
strain (what a perfect word!) of African-American song, where
the singer's ownership of his own suffering — in the absence of
all other property — burns at white heat (fire follows its own,
reverse color scheme). This quality is best referred back to the
melancholy hue altogether more natural than black or white,
a color suffusing the whole sky, covering all nature, human or
otherwise, including (as we have seen) the vast majority of songs:
blue. To sing the blues has been a historical necessity at all times
and in all places, Gilgamesh, Job, Vidyakara, Ventadorn, Wang
Wei, Petrarch, Tennyson, right up to Robert Johnson and all
his musical progeny. In the checkered (yes, that means discrete

squares of black and white) history of the United States, lament
has been a mode of expressive necessity for African-Americans.
White folks who make music have "cottoned on" to the straightforward historical fact that black folks who make music know
all too well how to sing through their pain, *how to survive by
singing*. Thank goodness everybody suffers. It's only because
everybody suffers that anybody — including the young Paul and
John, starting out in Liverpool — could recognize a voice (like
Arthur Alexander's in "Anna," for example) that fully embodies
suffering.

For the Beatles, the only thing that mattered was to fully
embody suffering, along with its unlikely but inevitable bedfel-
low, ecstasy. "Hey Judie, Judie, Judie, Judie, Judie!" Paul's voice
turns black, turns blue, the larynx turns black and blue, the music
turns inward, and by the same movement (on his shoulder?!), the
singer reaches outward to pull us all — Jude, you, me, the Super
Bowl crowd, lock, stock, and barrel — bodily into the orbit of
his own ecstasy.

Here, at the tail end of his Beatles career, Paul has earned the
right to sing like a black man, a noble condition he had often
aspired to. It is the deep and vexing heraldry of rock 'n' roll
that white singers want to sound black while holding on to the
privilege of looking white, thereby avoiding the statistical prob-
ability of getting pulled over by a cop on a rainy night. We find
ourselves once more thrust back upon the disturbing fact of
art's incapacity to effect any substantive change of heart in those
who perpetrate real suffering. It is the offense of music that its
audible signs of goodness — its claims of empowerment against
suffering — are merely that: *just* signs, nothing more. How could
signs heard in a song (however just) ever redress the wrongs they
point to, whether the wrongs are personal or universal, selfishly
or compassionately conceived? How could a song ever turn the
world into a *just place*? This ethical dream clamors to be heard,
its tenuous hold on reality carefully assessed.

II. NO VACANCY AT THE
HOLIDAY IN MUSIC

Once we've learned what it feels like to earn a song through the act of singing it, we become better equipped to sniff out anything less than that: the cheap, the sentimental, the unearned (these are all synonyms). Some years ago, I was driving through the Shenandoah Valley with a couple of good friends. It was my turn at the wheel and we were listening to pop radio, talking up a storm, solving life's riddles as they can only be solved on a road trip. Up on the air popped Whitney Houston singing her biggest hit, "The Greatest Love of All" (1986). Inexorably — as it still does every day, dozens of times, on radio stations across the country — the music changed key and reached its grand climax, Whitney wailing all the while. I groaned aloud in aesthetic agony. My friend Bill is never one to let me get away with such pomposity without giving some account (he calls me "the pomposer"). He challenged me to explain my obvious physical and moral distress. "What's the problem?" Bill asked. "What sin is this song committing?" I stopped groaning, paused to think for a moment, and then intoned, "It achieves apotheosis without struggle." Only a few times in one's life does one achieve such a peak of aphoristic insight without struggle. Again, it's only on a road trip that these spiritual breakthroughs can ever occur. It's because I was with friends, listening to a really bad hit song on the car radio, that I was vouchsafed this negative artistic truth, the core concept of this chapter. Whitney Houston — who elsewhere proves herself to be one of the best translators of the African-American church singing tradition into pop music — disgraces her vocation in "The Greatest Love" by turning the steady, holy ascent of a gospel voice into a precipitous, meteoric travesty. Her misdemeanor is all the more egregious considering how much the lyrics of the song have at stake (nothing less than the future of the human race). The final chorus embarrasses everything in sight — the songwriters, the original recording artist George Benson (whose fine version was released in 1977), the listener, and most of all Houston herself. She exploits the rich gospel sonority of her voice to perpetrate a false elevation of feeling without the requisite effort of ascending to that level. In its abrupt achievement of glory — nothing but sound and over-produced fury — this song defines *sentimentality*: sentiment unearned, feeling pretended to, emotion falsified through empty gesture, exaggeration, or unwarranted expression.

It does not excuse either Houston or the producers of this version of the song that the same depressing phenomenon of "apotheosis without struggle" characterizes much pop music. Given the intrinsic quality of the song (especially in Benson's original rendering), the authentic sentiment it is rooted in (one of the songwriters giving hopeful testimony against her fatal breast cancer), and the wild talent of Whitney Houston, the cheap thrill of this recording's full-throttle climax is an outrage.

"C'mon, Doctor Rose, it's just a pop song." That's what I occasionally hear from students when I get on my high horse like this. Might not, after all, my disdain for the song be just a matter of taste? That would be a far cry from the serious ethical lapse I am calling it to account for. Naturally, I could be wrong; after all, Whitney Houston's "The Greatest Love of All" was hugely popular, an overwhelmingly affecting triumph to its countless millions of fans.

I want to be absolutely clear about my intentions on this score. When I attack the song, or any song, for not having earned its emotions, it is not out of either pomposity (Bill knows this) or cynicism. On the contrary, *I am attacking the song for its own pomposity and cynicism.* "Pomp" signifies an outward display of ceremony, without any necessary correspondence of inner feeling. The "cynic," like the maligned dog (*cynos*), expresses affection towards its master only to achieve a base end. In the dog's case, it's a doggie biscuit; in the song's case, it's *ka-ching, ka-ching.* "The Greatest Love of All" is pompous and cynical, reaching its unworthy apotheosis without due struggle. As for the song's inordinate popularity: I blame Whitney for this phenomenon, not her fans. In this instance, she takes an Antoinette view of them and "lets them eat cake," instead of the nourishing stuff of her finest work. I am being so hard on her because she's so *good* — I could impose the same unreasonable critique on the later Paul McCartney, too.

Historically, artistic failures of this kind assume much greater import when they collide with the political realm. Leni Riefensthal's infamous, Nazi-celebrating film *The Triumph of the Will* proves beyond any doubt that a well-made work of art can lack any conscience. Riefensthal's filmmaking is of a piece with the Third Reich: the movie, like every piece of Nazi ideology, exploits symbols with absolute cynicism, drawing upon the spiritual energy of cultural forms (for example, the magnificent civic space of medieval Nuremberg) without the least intention of internalizing the process that evolved those beautiful forms in the first place. It is impossible to say anything meaningful about Nazi art, for it is precisely *meaningless.*

The same vacuum of meaning applies to the Nazi Holocaust. Primo Levi encapsulates this brutal point in an anecdote from his time at Auschwitz. One freezing day, in desperate thirst, he reached through the barred window of his barracks to break an icicle off the sill, so that he might suck on it. Just as he grasped it, an SS guard knocked it out of his hand. In despair, Levi could not help croaking, "*Warum?* [Why?]" The guard snapped, "*Hier ist kein Warum.* [Here there is no why.]"

In the strict physical sense, work is defined as a force demanding an exertion of energy exactly equal to the resultant movement of the object worked upon. Violence precludes this equation, for an object cannot be moved if it is merely destroyed. Violence is so *easy* because it calls for no work whatsoever. The force is already there, like mindless gravity, unearned, always ready to be unleashed, and utterly killing. Think of those twin towers, collapsing like so many straws. Like decks of cards. Easy. All too easy.

I am working to define *work* so carefully, in order that the work my chosen composers are doing may be understood in its authentic light: as the most important sort of work a person can do. It could well seem perverse to ask music lovers to conceive of "Hey Jude," or Beethoven's Ninth, or Schumann's Second, as *work*, even though they are commonly called "works." For many folks, the motivation for listening to these pieces arises in large measure from the acute and blissful break they grant from doing work. We could negotiate the terms of a feudal agreement on this point, consigning the work of construction to the serf-artists, leaving us lordly listeners free to enjoy the products of their labor, without having to do any work ourselves. Two even more unbalanced myths of artistic exchange also persist: first, that the artist — to our unwholesome delectation — sacrifices himself through overwork (Irving Stone's biographical novels of Michelangelo and Van Gogh) or second, that the artist doesn't have to do any work at all, but simply takes it down in dictation from God (Peter Shaffer's *Amadeus*).

I seek a new myth for art, and thereby, a new relation between music and listeners. To ensure that my own *mythopoeia* has more *sophia* and less *moria* in it, a few definitions are in order.

About pleasure, to begin with . . .

Pleasure differs from *diversion*, in the same way that a *holiday* differs from a *vacation*.

Pleasures and holidays saturate pockets of existence with value. Pleasures push us further into the puzzle and bustle of life, even to the point of propagating it anew. Through our pleasures, we dedicate ourselves to life. Holidays punctuate the calendar in rhythm with the seasons, satisfying our longing for patterns of meaningful change and recurrence. When we ride out into the countryside for a picnic or mark a radical break in history on Christmas or Passover, our conscious sense of Sabbath-taking belongs to a cycle of rest and renewal. The drama continues unbroken, though often submerged, when we return to work.

Without exception, official holidays commemorate some

work, some dedicated act, or some suffering, performed by others who came before us. Even birthdays implicitly acknowledge our mothers' labor. I can state the essential wisdom of chapters' worth of God's word in the Torah while standing one foot: festivals mean more when the work they interrupt is itself a pleasure.

On the other hand, and far less blithely, we design our diversions and vacations to be as stunning a rupture as possible from the pressing demands of our work. The drama is given over entirely to discontinuity: we remove ourselves as forcefully, as willfully, as we can from the perceived prison of our workplaces. A vacation grants us time off from the quest to define our role in the world, and we are terribly grateful for its clearance of our responsibilities, its temporary emptying-out of our data banks. Diversions stifle our hunger for meaning by foreclosing thought and feeling altogether. Along with their respite, diversions bring a genuine foretaste of death, which excuses us from all earthly relations.

One person's pleasure is another's diversion. For its true fans, baseball is always a pleasure, always an ascent, never a diversion (a player goes *up* to bat). Drugs are always a detour from pleasure, even from fully enjoying those art works created under their happy influence (Coleridge's "Kubla Kahn," the entire *Sgt. Pepper* album). A lot of music can be loved as both pleasure and diversion — the Beatles, for instance. With Beethoven, the territory of diversion is limited to pieces written expressly for *divertissement* (folk song arrangements, dances, etc.). Otherwise, Beethoven allows for no vacancy at the holiday in music he is always setting before us. He insists that we take *pleasure* in him, or else get the hell out and go listen to his silly contemporary Rossini instead. For some classical-music lovers Rossini's music actually scores a higher pleasure than Beethoven's; perhaps this is because Rossini is more forgiving towards our need for diversion, and he exploits that need, harnesses it, and finally releases it into pleasure. For me, the two composers are just two very different pleasures — as different from each other as the south wind and the northern lights.

III. romantic versus Romantic

The etymologies of the words *holiday* and *vacation* convey everything I have just painstakingly proposed, but with the amazing nutshell effect that typifies word origins. Holidays *make holy*; vacations *make empty*. Both activities are necessary for human life, both valuable. My claim is that certain works of music demand the first mode over the second, even if they lend themselves to both.

A single feeling, above all, generates the sense of holiness that distinguishes a holiday from other days, or from vacations. Whether it's Christmas or Hanukkah, Ramadan or Yom Kippur, Diwali or the Day of the Dead, every holiday is an act of *thanksgiving*. When you're on vacation, the only thing you are grateful for is that you're not working. When you are on holiday, you are thankful for every little thing, thankful most of all for the big things, for the source of the bounty holidays set forth and uphold.

In religious practice, everyone knows who that Source is and what is owed to Him (Her, Them). In music, however — including the religious kind — sources are manifold, and acknowledgments various. Even while a sacred work by Mozart explicitly praises God, it also *implicitly* praises Handel, Gluck, Haydn, and a host of other influences taken up and distilled through Mozart's imagination.

According to my hypothesis in the Preface (and to the available historical evidence), the robust evolution of secular instrumental music throughout the Enlightenment parallels the growing self-consciousness of humanistic — rather than theological — influences on cultural productions of every kind. One audible sign of symphonic music's evolving spiritual energy — what I call its *work* — is that the gratitude a composer feels for his musical forbears becomes mixed with an attitude of *debt*: a consciousness of the burden of the past. The determination and stress a composer feels about staying true to his technical models serve as the paradoxical marks of his spiritual liberation. The composer is set free to innovate by virtue of holding fast to tradition.

In the nineteenth century, these acts of faithful thanksgiving tendered by a composer to his beloved mentors in a piece of music become more and more anxious, to the degree that the composer feels more and more *belated*. The worst feeling an artist can have is that his or her work stands as a mere postscript to a breakthrough achieved by a past master. This was the nightmare scenario for Romantic composers, every one of whom either felt, or stubbornly refused to feel, belated after Beethoven. One way or another, they all staked their claims in his musical shadow.

The literary critic Harold Bloom's most famous book (among the incredible hundreds of his publications), called *The Anxiety of Influence*, proposes a "positive feedback loop" for such artistic *angst*. Its Freudian insight is that a poet, out of a vast, productive anxiety, acknowledges the spiritual source of her own poem by deliberately and more or less obviously *killing* that source. Bloom devises an entire lexicography of Greek terms for such acts of creative violence, which are irresistible to academics for their classical and theological bite. Ironically, generations of scholars have appropriated Bloom's terminology without any anxiety about his influence whatsoever. I gratefully acknowledge Bloom's help, even as I turn aside from his Oedipal vortex to more Mosaic ground (which he magisterially covers elsewhere).

Composers pay homage to their influences by *arguing* with them. Robert Schumann's Second Symphony is an argument about music with Bach, with Haydn, with Beethoven, with Berlioz, with Mendelssohn, reaching a thrilling climax of audible argumentation in the last movement. In effect, Schumann argues with the entire history of music, especially his nemesis Beethoven.

If Schumann already felt belated towards Beethoven, imagine how Brahms felt in the next generation (no need to imagine this, just *listen* to his First Symphony); imagine how Mahler felt in the next, occupied as he often was with conducting Beethoven and

Brahms symphonies, and even recomposing Schumann's. Then there is the entire panorama of twentieth-century symphonic music: Ives, Schoenberg, Bartók, Shostakovich, Stockhausen, Rochberg, Harbison. Each one of these more or less pugnacious masters stands in the ring with Beethoven and goes 15 rounds, giving back to Beethoven as good as he gets, punch-drunk with love and *angst*. Composers who are foolhardy enough to write symphonies in the twenty-first century are still feeling it. Imagine how I feel. You don't have to, for I am telling you.

It's not that Beethoven is the only problem; after all, even *he* felt belated, especially towards Handel in his last years. It's that Beethoven is the *avatar* of the problem, the demigod-made-man, the Promethean figure who brings down an Olympian musical fire that not only sings, but singes. Beethoven was the first one of us who ever felt any real anxiety towards his own craft, who made the first probing *critique* of his own tradition. The philosopher Theodor Adorno writes beautifully about these matters in the fragmentary manuscript for his unfinished *Beethoven*.

What to do, what to do about Beethoven's influence? *That* is the question fanning the flames of the symphonic tradition after the Ninth Symphony, a paramount stylistic problem that makes the Romantic symphony such a dramatic and unsettling field of inquiry. And it is what helps to make the word "Romantic" the single most misunderstood word in the history of the arts.

Whenever I plunge into musical Romanticism with students, I make a distinction between *Romantic* (with a capital "R") and *romantic* (with the lowercase "r"). Strange to say, the meanings of the two terms are nearly opposite in their emotional vectors and psychological impacts. "Isn't it romantic?" (one of my favorite songs by Rodgers and Hart) rhetorically inquires about the lowercase phenomena: "music in the night, a dream that can be heard . . . breezes playing in the trees above . . . sweet symbols in the moonlight." Valentine-card sentiments, every one of them. Lorenz Hart was a master of transfiguring such clichés, which always answer a desire, fulfill a pledge, realize a dream.

"Is it Romantic?" is a question Rodgers and Hart do not address — for good reason, for it can be a terrifying query. From Goethe's Werther to Coleridge's Ancient Mariner, from Keats's Hyperion to Byron's Manfred, from Percy Shelley's Prometheus to Mary Shelley's Frankenstein, Romantic literature delivers one stunning blow after another to "romantic" self-satisfaction, demonstrating with diabolical certitude that *no desire can ever be answered, no pledge ever fulfilled, no dream ever realized.*

This raging dissatisfaction with life's illusions, this *poetics of disappointment* (the title of an excellent book on the Romantic poetic tradition by Laura Quinney), is a far cry from the popular notion of what is "romantic," including the Romantic symphony. Any "open-hearted surgery" practiced upon beloved works of nineteenth-century symphonic music would prove that every one of them bravely bears the capital "R" on its heart as well as on its sleeve, a blazon of Romantic fury and passionate unease. Berlioz's *Symphonie fantastique,* Mendelssohn's "Scottish," the Schumann C Major we'll take up — in every one of these symphonies, the composer goes as wandering spirit, lost in a real or imagined landscape haunted by ghosts of one kind or another (Beethoven, for one). In the next generation, this searching becomes yet more intense: Brahms, Tchaikovsky, Bruckner, and Dvorak are all committed to finding out where they come from, where they stand, and how to make a home on that musical ground. Through a variety of crises, these belated Romantics demonstrate their ultimate homelessness, the mounting certainty that the only condition under which they feel at home is *wandering,* movement by movement, through every region of the heart's perplexity.

So how is it that so many fans of Romantic symphonies are able to embrace these unnerving works as "romantic," as background music to provide a nice atmosphere for a candlelight supper? Are such romantics merely inattentive to Romantic music's darker aspects? Or is there something intrinsic to these works that lends itself so readily and popularly to passive *diversion* instead of fully engaged *pleasure*, as I have defined these at some length? How is it that the spiritual *dissatisfaction* of Romantic music is so easily *satisfying* to a casual listener?

I do not have an answer. It would be disingenuous of me to offer one, since I have been guilty of such "abuses" of Romantic music throughout my adult life. I have wooed with Tchaikovsky's "Winter Dreams" as well as with wine. It is possible that the capital offense of appropriating Romantic music for romantic purposes is so common and so effective because we can, in an unconscious way, "scapegoat" the composer: we send him out into the wilderness of his self-examination, into his ordeal of testing and destroying one illusion after another. Consequently, we ourselves are able to experience that arduous journey at an aesthetic distance, safe in the arms of our beloved. In other words, the Romantic symphony offers the supreme Aristotelian *catharsis*, tempering our passion by audibly exorcising its authentic, darker face.

That's all well and good, especially where I live in Tennessee, where fully embodying the passions of a Romantic symphony might get a body shot full of holes. But now let's close the distance and go out into the wilderness with one of these composers. Let's see what it feels like to be the scapegoat and wield the axe alongside him, knocking down illusions to make way for new myths. It's no candlelight supper, let alone a picnic. But maybe you should grab that bottle of wine on your way out. Every Romantic worth the name is always busy, frantic, ingenious, turning wildernesses into festivals.

IV. ROBERT SCHUMANN THROWS A PARTY

We are talking now of symphonic finales, so successfully disguised by Romantic composers as triumphs of the spirit. In the meantime, as they go, unfolding moment by moment, these final movements sustain an agony of uncertain outcome, an inventory of missteps, turnings back, crushing doubts, maniacal forays into danger, repeated and thwarted attempts to break through, all of which cannot merely be "resolved" by a final cadence, however triumphant that may be. What matters to Beethoven in his Ninth (the Romantic model) and Schumann in his Second (the arch-Romantic experiment) is the succession of trials, *the dreadful possibility of defeat*, never the final verdict, happy as that may seem. The steep ascent is what heats the blood, increases the pulse, hastens the breathing through the clambering, sometimes hardscrabble, act of "singing." The ultimate arrival at the summit leaves the audience cold — that is why we must clap our hands at the end, for sheer animal warmth, having been abandoned at such a rare height by the composer.

Attending symphony concerts has always been a hardship for me. To sit still among polite concertgoers during a performance of Schumann's Second — in which every phrase demands to be sung aloud, every crescendo sets in motion a comparable expansion of my own ungainly frame, every crisis in the music propels an untoward, maniacal reaction in my awkward limbs — is as impossible for me as repressing the upward turn of my smile when my wife or one of my children walks into the room. And then, to applaud the conductor and orchestra — as if that cracking, high-pitched noise could account for the depths of feeling undergone, or could do justice to the composer, whose name at least ought to be shouted once or twice, up into the rafters of the concert hall, in simple gratitude . . . well, I just can't do it. But of course, I *do* do it; I could hardly stay away, when I make concert attendance a requirement in my Vanderbilt courses. I am therefore relieved that I can settle down with you now, in the last half of this chapter, to enjoy the finale of Schumann's Second without worrying about the inevitability — if we were sitting listening to these pieces next to each other in a concert hall — of kicking you in the shins with my flying foot, or knocking the wind out of you with my wayward elbow.

We will make our way into Schumann's universe of complex

allusions by way of a pair of popular songs. I recently mentioned to my freshman seminar students a favorite pop song of
mine, "The Way It Is," by Bruce Hornsby and the Range, from
their eponymous 1986 album. They all knew the song, but only
because they know a hip-hop song by 2Pac from the mid-1990s
called "Changes," which heavily "samples" Hornsby's song from
the decade before. One student told me that he had downloaded
the original Hornsby, just to hear what 2Pac's "Changes" really
were. He was "totally disappointed." The experience of the sam-
pled hip-hop version made Hornsby's original fall flat.

We are in Harold Bloom territory here. One of the pillars of
his theory about the anxiety of influence is that poets overcome
their anxiety about masterworks through ingenious acts of paro-
dying them. The apprentice submits the master's work to radical
metamorphosis, revealing new and untapped potential lying
dormant within it. The apprentice thereby knocks the stuffing
out of the master, takes him down a peg, beats him at his own
game — in short, becomes the master.

Bloom applies a theological term for these acts of parody:
kenosis, the Catholic belief in *the emptying-out of Christ's divinity* so that He might die on the cross and redeem humanity. The
Incarnation knocked the divine stuffing out of Jesus of Nazareth,
so that he (lowercase "h" now) could be taken down by pegs, oh
those awful pegs.

Whatever was luminous, fresh, or possibly divine in Bruce
Hornsby's "The Way It Is" (a song about social injustice) is
mischievously undone by the hip-hop twists and turns 2Pac
subjects it to. Eighties pop music always lived on the edge of
the ridiculous (the movie *Music and Lyrics* makes hay out of
this fact). Hornsby is an easy target for the smart, sassy 2Pac's
ironic machinations. Moreover, the young man Tupac Amaru
Shakur — who was fatally shot in a drive-by incident at the age
of 25 — had firsthand experience of the racism Hornsby's song
poignantly addresses — a plight that the white Hornsby can only
imagine. All these factors — especially our archetypal shift of a

white voice into black, in order to turn it blue — make 2Pac's sampling of the "The Way It Is" strangely more authentic than the original version. 2Pac's unsettling palimpsest obscures Hornsby's template in a brilliant, brutal act of musical *kenosis*. That student of mine will probably never be able to enjoy Hornsby's song on its pristine ground, so dissatisfying is it to him after his loss of innocence at the hands of the smart, sly, and possibly divine hip-hop version.

Now let's turn to the opening music of the first movement of Schumann's Second Symphony (a prelude to our focus on its finale). Schumann "samples" the opening motto of Franz Josef Haydn's last and greatest symphony, the "London" Symphony, making "changes" on it that render Haydn almost unrecognizable. He plays 2Pac to Haydn's Hornsby, transforming his model by way of *understatement*. Instead of the majestic, voluminous statement Haydn gives his motto in the *tutti* orchestra, Schumann "knocks the stuffing" out of the motto and gives it to quiet trumpets, shorn of their usual majestic, *forte* character. The trumpets play Haydn's motto as demure "background music" to Schumann's flowing, sweeping string lines in the foreground.

The presence of Haydn's motto at the beginning of Schumann's Second had to be pointed out to me by a professor when I was an undergraduate studying the Romantic symphony. It was definitely a "huh?" moment for me, something I could not fully appreciate because my listening was not yet grounded in the Classic works of Haydn or Mozart from the eighteenth century. Schumann *expects* us to recognize his quotation of Haydn. To his Romantic sensibility (vintage 1846), it is a thoroughly audible sign of Classicism (vintage 1795). For him, it is meant to be a "duh!" moment. One could not ask for a more typical instance of the Classic imagination than the opening motto of the "London" Symphony, with its synthesis of conventionality and surprise. Schumann is counting on our recognition of the motto, so that we can appreciate the changes he is wreaking upon it and thereby hear how he *appreciates* Haydn (literally, *increases*

Haydn's value), reshaping the Classic motto to the point where it becomes Romantic.

Once the listening mind grasps the "obvious" Haydn connection at the start of Schumann's Second Symphony (this is what music professors get paid for), the listening heart can make two great leaps:

  a) Wow, that motto sounds so *different* from the way it sounds in Haydn!
  b) Wow, that motto sounds so much *better* than the way it sounds in Haydn!

Better? Wouldn't this, again, be just a matter of taste — as with fried chicken, a choice between the Haydn "original" and the Schumann "extra crispy"? Besides, no one has ever made the claim (nor could they) that Schumann's Second is a better symphony than Haydn's "London."

Still, in the first moments of its sounding, the Second Symphony of Robert Schumann performs a magical transformation of Haydn, giving the old master's motto an aura of mystery, sweetness and modesty that is so deeply affecting because it could not possibly have been anticipated as a consequence of the original motto. Schumann's version of the Haydn is "better" *because it is different.* Where Haydn's motto was purposely pompous, Schumann's is introspective. Where Haydn was regal, Schumann is reverent. Where Haydn was just (*giusto*), Schumann is merciful. The quality of the motto is not strained by its trumpets, as it was in Haydn's orchestra; "it droppeth as the gentle rain from heaven," in a flowing, exalted melodic line never imagined by Haydn.

Above all, Schumann's version "improves" upon Haydn's because it is no longer merely speaking of its own grand accord (as Haydn does), but is rather *speaking to Haydn*, reaching out to dear, beloved Papa, in loving retrospection, reverence and un(re)-strained appeal for mercy from the master. Whereas Haydn takes an objective gesture of public ceremony (the grandiose motto) and makes it *subjective*, Schumann takes Haydn's magnificent assertion of subjectivity and makes it *intersubjective*. What stood in perfect autonomy (the proud motto, played by Haydn's *tutti*) now stands in mild, deferential relation, the sign of a grateful, *anxious* love tendered by belated apprentice to forgiving master.

The intersubjectivity of this music doesn't stop here, for the opening counterpoint of the symphony — between flowing string lines and trumpet motto — has a profounder source: J. S. Bach looms over this *Introduzione*, the presiding spirit for its disposition of parts, even unto the sweet, Baroque contours of the strings. The strategy of placing Haydn's motto in the background comes from Bach, too: in his chorale preludes and fantasies, the borrowed tune — the "chorale," a tune in some cases composed by Martin Luther himself — is often relegated to a subordinate position, submitting to Bach's newly invented counterpoints. All you have to do is pay attention to "Jesu, Joy of Man's Desiring" next time you're at a wedding, and you will hear this relation between Bach's flowing "modern" music up front and his stately "ancient" source taking up the rear.

This undermining of source by commentary in Bach — whereby the old Lutheran hymn becomes a series of intermittent cues for Bach's own virtuosity — cannot be accounted for by Bloom's notion of "anxiety." In Bach, the presence of Luther's chorale melody is the *only reason for this music's being*. A chorale prelude serves precisely as a *prelude* to the congregational singing of the Lutheran chorale. Why would Bach undercut the primacy of the hymn, thrusting his own invention into the musical foreground? The chutzpah is an audible sign of his overarching love for the source, a measure of his desire to ornament the pristine chorale with his finest and most complex filigree work, even to the point of overwhelming the original with his own design.

Bach's tone of unadulterated celebration was long gone by the time Schumann set his sights on Haydn's motto. To reiterate my melancholy Romantic plaint: it is *belatedness* that sets the tone for Schumann's Second Symphony. What other masters of symphonic composition could make an apprentice feel so *late* in the day as Vater Bach and Papa Haydn, who both wrought so many miracles so long ago, in a different world, a different century, a different *ethos* altogether for music-making? Two hundred and fifty cantatas! One hundred and four symphonies! *One hundred and four*, for God's sake, literally for *His* sake! (Bach and Haydn both inscribed *ad gloriam Dei* on their works.) What's a belated Romantic composer with chronic writer's block like Schumann to do in the face of such achievements?

He does the only thing he can do. He sticks in his thumb and pulls out a plum. Schumann is *hungry* for Haydn, so he must have him . . . but only on his own terms, only by ripping Haydn's motto from its source and changing its nature utterly, by way of Johann Sebastian Bach's contrapuntal art.

We are nowadays very familiar with this epoch-jumbling technique of multiple stylistic reference, quotation and appropriation. It currently goes by the name of "postmodernism." But it was *Romanticism* in the first place. Still, there is a vast difference in spirit between the Romantic triangle *Schumann/Haydn/Bach* and the postmodern triangle (for instance) *Philip Glass/Vivaldi/thirteenth-century Notre Dame Cathedral polyphony*, the musical *ménage à trois* of Glass's recent soundtrack to the film *The Illusionist*. Philip Glass is not so much hungry for his historical sources as he is *bored by them*, turning his boredom to good account by exaggerating it, and thus elevating it to one or more Francophone conditions, variously called *ennui, malaise, anomie*, etc. Glass's music — a more pretentious cousin to Whitney Houston's *débâcle* — is an audible sign of our era's lousy psychological need to motivate and justify our emotional inertia, as if by magic. By definition, *magic* describes anything that effects change through insubstantial illusion and *no work at all*. That is why Glass's soundtrack for *The Illusionist* may be the perfect realization of Glass's spellbinding art.

Schumann was ill-equipped to practice such legerdemain. Rather than pull a rabbit out of a hat, poor Robert would have walked miles into the Rhenish countryside to track one down in its native habitat. Schumann is *famished* for experience, hell-bent on substituting experience for what he knows to be a fatal innocence. He is ready to work for every particle of it. But why should Schumann be so ravenous, so all-consuming in his desire to *have* Haydn — not merely to take possession of his legacy, but to take control of him, by transforming him? *Integrity* an old-fashioned word, but I think it fits in this case. Its sense has always been radical. Integrity means *wholeness*, as integers are whole numbers. The Hebrew word *shalom* means precisely "wholeness," and by extension "peace." It is what Jews wish each other in greeting, also upon the stranger, even upon the enemy in a perfect Talmudic universe. Another word for wholeness is *sanity*. Schumann knows that to be whole, to be sane as a composer of symphonies — to have any peace of mind about his undertaking — he must make a reckoning of tradition, of Haydn, of Bach, of the whole nine centuries, if truth be told. The Second Symphony's opening combination of Bach and Haydn turns out to be a polyphonic texture going back to the eleventh century — to the invention of polyphony itself.

Sanity was no mere artistic abstraction for poor Schumann, who died in an insane asylum after several suicide attempts. Holding himself together was always an act of clinical near-impossibility. The miracle of his best music is that it often works restoratively for Schumann as a means of productively distributing his soul into its irreconcilable component parts — into his notorious alter egos Florestan and Eusebius, to name two, but into a host of others as well, including Haydn and Bach. The opening of the Second Symphony confronts the fragility of individual selfhood. On our behalf, Schumann stakes the individual's personal claims in the face of those Others who constantly inhabit his imagination and inhibit his self-certainty. The predicament is ours, too, not Schumann's alone. Our integrity is at stake as well as his. His Second Symphony can be our ally in these lifelong acts of self-possession, of self-realizing integration.

My composer friend John Harbison — whose wonderful music we will come to in the next chapter — was visiting Nashville once as our guest composer at the university, and we were driving to dinner in my car, talking and taking delight in our conversation as we always do, with the classical radio station inadvertently left on from earlier in the day. All at once, the announcer said, "And now, Robert Schumann's Symphony No. 2 in C Major, performed by Wolfgang Zawallisch conducting the Dresden State Orchestra" (remarkable, this central importance of car music in my life). John and I stopped talking and just *listened* to those stunning first seconds of the piece, the simultaneous flow of strings and leap of quiet trumpets. I was doubly unnerved: in the first place by the audible alliance of *Schumann/Haydn/Bach* and in the second by the presence in my passenger seat of one of the best living composers. I couldn't say anything. At last, John did. As Schumann's *Introduzione* wended its way towards the *Allegro* of the first movement, John quietly remarked, "You know, you can hear just what this music cost him." I blurted, "Yes, you can, yes!" and then just kept my eyes on the road. Harbison had reaffirmed for me what I already knew, but did not have the words to understand. In the car, listening to Schumann together, my friend John had restored to me my calling, my responsibility as a composer, my charge for writing this book someday, so that I could see it plain and see it whole.

In the inner movements of the Second Symphony, Schumann offers two exciting Romantic experiments in *turning song into symphony*. A basic flaw exists in this enterprise: it can't be done. No good way has ever been found of turning song into symphony. Oh, songs are songs, and symphonies are symphonies, and never the main shall tweet. The song "Hey Jude" *is* what it is, just the song it needs to be. Alas, the same cannot be said for Paul McCartney's misbegotten *Liverpool Oratorio* and *Standing Stone*, both mangled attempts to aggrandize simple song into muddleheaded, hydra-composed symphony (poor fellow, he needed lots of ghostwriting). With a good deal more *pathos* and self-reliance, Schumann gave the chimerical, alchemical notion of turning song into symphony his best shot in these inner Scherzo and Adagio movements of the Second. Like McCartney, he was a consummate songwriter, so there was some chance of pulling it off; moreover, unlike McCartney, he could actually read music.

The Scherzo (second movement) has an impossible-to-sing main theme with a relentless drive. This manic stuff serves as the frame for two slower, singing interludes, which rise up like habitable islands out of the ocean of Schumann's restlessness. Nothing can remain still in this wild, roiling sea — including those brief respites of song. The movement's whole humor is one of pique, of coherent thought threatened by Schumann's native state of distraction. After all, Scherzo means "joke" in Italian. From Beethoven on, a symphonic Scherzo often comes across as a very practical joke, deployed for letting off unmanageable steam. At the tail end of Schumann's Scherzo, Haydn's motto makes a quick and nasty cameo, sounding like a slap upside Schumann's head for having so naïvely proposed to sing two Lieder in the middle of a symphony — a pathetic collapse by the composer to his default mode of composing songs.

On the other hand (vocal cord?), the Adagio (third movement) of this symphony carves a vast space for singing out of its quarry of woe. This fine, lamenting song stretches into a superhuman arc, as only violins can stretch. Bach's Baroque countenance shines forth again at a crucial point, as a literal counterpoint to Schumann's vehement singing. It is of great and perverse courage on Schumann's part to be thus continually reproaching himself in the audible presence of his more judicious heroes, for the sin of subjecting song to the inhospitable environment of symphony. It is as if a wild palomino had somehow got a bit in its mouth: the song runs free, right into the harness of symphonic form. Poor song.

Both versions of Schumann's would-be *song-into-symphony*

— Scherzo and Adagio — must be provisional. As I have said, it is impossible to turn a song into a symphony. *It can't be done.* Schumann splendidly violates both compositional principles in making the experiment. Indeed, we know from Beethoven that proposing to convert a song — or even an ode — into a symphony is risky, messy, downright foolhardy, as any soprano who has had to sing the unconscionably high notes in the finale of the Ninth will tell you. Spanning the breadth of the lyrical nineteenth century, the heroic efforts of Franz Schubert and Piotr Ilych Tchaikovsky to convert their singing into symphony-making are magnificent failures *as such*; their symphonies remain lovable and indispensable on account of the dramatic ways in which their native modes of lyricism disintegrate, in the free-ion environment of symphonic development.

Against such odds (Beethoven's Ninth, above all), Schumann decides he has nothing to lose. In the finale of the Second Symphony, he takes a discontinuous, evolutionary leap and proposes something unheard before, in fact unheard of. More thrilling, we can actually hear the new idea take shape in the first few minutes of the finale, emerging as a new species of symphony, via a natural selection of adaptive traits from preceding life forms. The new, healthy creature who emerges from the slime of Schumann's previously rueful singing now has an unprecedented vitality, an utterly new complexion, all the more unlikely in its vigor because it reverses the preceding natural order. Since a song will not find a way to adapt into a symphony, *Schumann forces the symphony to adapt into song.*

There may also be a pedagogical model for what's going on at the start of this finale. My daughter repeatedly complains to me how her high-school math teacher insists on her *showing him her work* when solving a problem of geometry or calculus. Likewise, Schumann is answerable to the symphonic calculus set forth by his teachers (Haydn, Mendelssohn, and Beethoven), and prudently decides to show them his work. In the process, the composer shows *us* his work, too.

The feeling abides in the Second Symphony's finale — as it has from the very beginning of the first movement — that we are tuning into a program already in progress, eavesdropping on a conversation long underway between Schumann and his *daimones*, those attending musical spirits who were always whispering in his ear (see Chapter 5) — all the more vividly on account of Schumann's ongoing pathological condition of hallucinating disembodied voices.

In short, we hear Schumann doing his homework — that is, *working to come home* to the ground where he can take full possession of himself and own up to every part of his fractured, always singing nature. In this newfound home, Schumann can possess those insistent voices who haunt him, instead of merely being possessed by them.

What is the "new calculus" that Schumann proposes, then? What is the "differential" that effects the change between him and his masters, the entire lot of them, Bach, Haydn, Mozart, Beethoven, Schubert, and Mendelssohn? It's fun to extend the mathematical conceit, so let me show it to you this way:

$$\frac{dx}{dy} = \Delta x(n+1) = y$$

where x = symphony
y = song
n = the indeterminate influence of earlier composers

It is impossible to convert a song into a symphony ($dy/dx = 0$). Schumann tried that in the middle movements, and it yielded beautifully mixed fruits. So, instead of beating his head against that wall anymore, he blithely inverts the differential, and *converts symphony into song*.

Schumann's daring reaches its climactic perch right at the start of the finale. He throws all caution, all historical scruple, to the wind, throws open vast kegs of wine and beer — in short, he throws a party. Everybody is invited: you, me, the whole company of beloved symphonic masters. First of all, there is a bold knock at the door, a noble flourish, and in strides Schumann's friend and colleague, Felix Mendelssohn, the two of them bound by their shared mission to raise the cultural bar for German music in their generation. Felix presents his audible calling card, the motto of his famous "Italian" Symphony — and so the party begins with the clinking of glasses of red table wine all around. Gracious host that he is, Robert welcomes Felix with a great bear hug, helping the highly decorous, *haut-bourgeois* Mendelssohn to unwind a bit and feel at home in this somewhat shabbier space. Schumann bends Mendelssohn's Italian tune to his own goodwill, tilting it off-course from its lilting rectitude. By the time Schumann is finished with his grandiose *Wilkommen* of friend Felix, we are all now drinking fine old German beer, which beats that thin Italian stuff (let alone the cloying Sabbath wine of Mendelssohn's early childhood) any day.

In candid camaraderie, Schumann shares with Mendelssohn what he's been going through. He lays out the ordeal of singing the Adagio, even humming a few bars of the tune and rushing it terribly in the retelling — even singing it upside down on a high, wailing clarinet, a vexed travesty of its original lament. Robert confesses to Felix his failed effort to turn song into symphony (imagine that, the born Jew as Father Confessor). Schumann humbly acknowledges his friend's superior ingenuity in finding a balance between Romantic lyricism and Classic development (just listen to the "Italian" Symphony).

The alternation of Schumann's two parodies — of Mendelssohn and of himself — takes up this whole first section of the Finale, serving as a herald for the guest of honor, who is on his way — *you know who*, the one to whom so much is "ode," the fellow who first came up with the notion of a finale's bringing back tunes from earlier movements and explicitly rejecting them as inadequate to the task at hand. This intensely eloquent (though wordless!) strategy — invented by Beethoven in the Ninth and adapted here by Schumann in his Second — will become Gustav Mahler's symphonic signature in his Second, Third, Fourth, Fifth, Sixth, etc.

The *real presences* at this juncture of the Finale are even more palpable than in the Introduction of the first movement. Schumann is not just composing a Finale, he is composing a community. His simple wish that we recognize and welcome Mendelssohn — a special courtesy at a German party, in the light of Mendelssohn's Jewish birth — is on a par with his simple hope that we will welcome back his own Adagio tune, for which he makes a special apology. He distorts the original character of each borrowed tune just enough to light-heartedly mock them and force them to submit to the finale's party mood. We have all encountered manic party hosts like this, if not acted the part ourselves. The host tries just a bit too hard to make sure we're having a good time. His urgent directive to *celebrate* sweeps us up, draws us in, disarms us, converting all our "sounds of woe into hey, nonny, nonny." (It is impossible for me not to envision Emma Thompson slyly intoning this line, in Kenneth Branagh's film version of *Much Ado About Nothing* . . . she reads them from a book, in light-hearted mockery of Shakespeare, forcing the Bard to submit to the movie's party mood.)

Schumann even has the nerve to invoke Bach once more, summoning him to the festival out of his well-earned rest to help provoke a few dissonant Baroque rounds on the opening flourish of the movement. With so many party guests to attend to, how is the host supposed to manage symphonic structure at the same time? *It can't be done.* One darn impossibility after another: no way to make a reasonable wedding of song and symphony, no way to hold a structure together when there are so many presences to account for. Instead of despairing over this impossibility, Schumann has now learned the wisdom to accept it, to embrace it, *to relish it.* The music simply rises, rises, reaching a culminating shout of anticipatory celebration . . .

. . . and then, in an all-encompassing hush, it gives way

altogether — to what? To whom? Who *is* that in the open door-
way, who *is* that on the threshold, backlit by the glory of the
starry canopy? Who is it who now walks companionably in,
joining the party with a sweet nod of gratitude to the host and a
modest bow to the other guests?

It's not the Beethoven we might have reasonably expected.
With so many aspects of Schumann's Second depending on
Beethoven's Ninth Symphony, we might have felt sure of welcoming the Beethoven of the Ninth. But *that* Beethoven could not
be further from *this* Beethoven, the one who now walks through
the door: the lyrical Ludwig, who composed but one cycle of
songs, *An die ferne Geliebte*, on poems of Aloys Jeitelles, and
here we have the most beautiful one of that set, the sixth and
final one, the *envoi* sending forth songs of love to the "distant
beloved":

> *Take, then, these songs,*
> *That I to you, beloved, sang,*
> *Sing them again in the evenings*
> *To the sweet sounds of the lute!*
>
> *When the red twilight then moves*
> *toward the calm, blue lake,*
> *And the last ray dies*
> *behind that hilltop;*
>
> *And you sing, what I have sung,*
> *What I, from my full heart,*
> *Artlessly have sounded,*
> *Only aware of its longings.*
>
> *For before these songs yields,*
> *What separates us so far,*
> *And a loving heart reaches*
> *For what a loving heart has consecrated.*

"And you sing, what I have sung." The invitation Beethoven tenders could not be more open or more exacting. Could there be anyone more "distant" or more "beloved" than a composer of the next generation, doing his best to be faithful, to be a loving heart reaching for what a loving heart has consecrated? Schumann accepts Beethoven's invitation, and *sings what Beethoven has sung*, and also returns the favor, welcoming him to his party.

[Since it is my task in this book to dismantle unwarranted, *unearned* sentimentality, I will but briefly mention the particular poignancy this final song of *An die ferne Geliebte* must have had for Schumann, as he measured his distance from his beloved wife Clara, often geographical — so many trips from home for them both, especially for her as the most distinguished concert pianist of her time — and always psychological. How he struggled to stay sane with her, how mightily he strived!]

With Beethoven's arrival at the party — the full stop in the orchestra, the subsequent rising of Beethoven's song — all hope of salvaging Classic structure for this finale collapses. There is an exquisite irony in this turn of affairs: Schumann takes Beethoven at his word (at Schiller's word!) in the Ninth, but goes so much further than Beethoven ever imagined towards radically altering the nature of a symphonic finale and turning it into song. The melody of the "Ode to Joy" is not something that could be called "lyrical"; it is rather in the mode of hymnody — more specifically, of French Revolutionary hymnody, to which Beethoven paid special attention for its secular messianic vision. The Ode also smacks of military band music, and Beethoven certainly makes Turkish hash out of this connection. There's even a flavor of simplistic folk song in the Ode, which makes sense for *alle Menschen*. In the finale of the Ninth, we are much closer to a beer garden than a serenader's garden. What a mischievous twist it is for Schumann to *fulfill* Beethoven's mission in the Ninth, forcing his Second Symphony to surrender to the mandates of lyrical song, by way of an actual, full-fledged, Beethoven song — not a four-square ode, not a beer-guzzler's raucous strain, but a genuine *Lied*, an actual flight of sung Beethovenian melody, one of the only ones ever penned by the master, a gem from his lone song cycle.

In two great waves of song, the borrowed melody unfolds and metamorphoses at its own serenely impassioned pace. Schumann's party has reached that stage of gentle tipsiness where everyone is ready to sing the same song, but no one is quite steady enough to sing it together at the same time, or even in the same way. Just as he did with Mendelssohn's "Italian," Schumann makes Beethoven's melody into something entirely his own, changing its shape *just so* for the purposes of party singing, so that it is no longer a quotation, but rather adaptation, transformation — *hommage* (the extra "m" of the French word makes it perfect for wordless singing . . . for "hummage"). At first appearance, the tune rises in a straight line, rather than folding back on itself, as Beethoven would have it. As if in protest at this manipulation, the orchestra (Beethoven himself, perhaps, after a couple of beers?) explodes into an anxious set of rounds on the song's contour, at one point going the wrong way down in the cellos. But again, the music rises, rises (with more help from Bach's dissonant counterpoint), reaching again a culminating shout of anticipatory celebration . . .

. . . and then, in another all-encompassing hush, it gives way altogether — to what? To whom? Beethoven is already present and accounted for. Even if he's gone off in a huff to the loo (lots and lots of beer, remember), there is no need to shout him back through the door. Why so much fuss, why this second huge wave of anticipation and arrival? What gentle beast, its hour come round at last, slouches towards Schumann's party to be born . . .? (Even Yeats, for all his Crazy Jane songs, knew not what could emerge from an ordeal of psychic disintegration like Schumann's.)

. . . Schumann, that's who. For a few precious seconds, we hear the host singing in his own voice: a simple, unadorned song, emptied of all constraint, all urgency, all worry. There is something profoundly paradoxical going on here. At the very moment Schumann comes closest to copying the contour of Beethoven's melody outright, the metamorphosis stands complete: Schumann bursts out of his own chrysalis. It is by virtue of the absolute closeness of his relation to Beethoven's song that his own singing can now take flight. "Your song, what does it know?" That's what the poet/survivor Paul Celan asks after the Holocaust's horrors, when a song may well know nothing, not one damn thing (see Chapter 5). Robert Schumann, in his own time, through his own predicament, gives us a tentative answer to Celan at this momentary clearing in the forest of his symphonic music — not in words, but through a now-absolutely-lyrical orchestra:

If my song knows anything, it knows that whatever it knows must be paid for — not through self-destruction, but through self-sacrifice. Exacting that cost, my song then gives me back myself. At least for the moment.

This answer is all the more telling for its heartbreaking transience. Schumann sings in Beethoven's tones, smoothing out the roughness of the master's rhythm, letting all the notes of the song flow straight and sure, like a chorale prelude by Bach. Mendelssohn is not forgotten, either: here, if ever there was one, is a *Song without Words*, Felix's Romantic innovation charging Robert with the courage to proceed, the resolution to take hold of his own soul by remastering Beethoven's, through the unprecedented calculus of *converting a symphony into a song without words*.

And guess who shows up at the party, at the last minute . . . well, of course, you guessed it. The whole symphony, from first to last movement, has been playing a game of "Hadyn seek," Schumann's quest to do something worthy of Papa Haydn, who has been hidin' in the next room the whole time, listening carefully to what's been going on, leisurely drinking his own six-pack (that's the number of symphonies he could write for a single London season). Now he marches through the door — on the truepenny motto from the "London" symphony — laughing and bellowing with pleasure at his prodigal son Robert's homecoming. Haydn places a gold star at last on Schumann's homework, ruffling Robert's hair in pure affection (a nice change from his earlier slap upside the head).

The feeling of joyous approbation — of benediction — at Haydn's last-minute arrival is so overwhelming that we, as listeners, are called upon to consider whether this final appearance of the motto is a triumph of historical imagination or a gratuitous act of cyclic neatness and wishful thinking. I think I understand those many orchestral musicians, conductors, and fans of Romantic music who dismiss the finale of Schumann's Second as an unholy mess. I only hope that this chapter will help them to see that it is a holy mess.

How can I know if I am right in imagining Schumann throwing a party? I do not. It's a ludicrous notion, I know it is. Fortunately, I have a friend — a Lennon to my doubting McCartney — who urged me to let go of my doubts about using the crazy idea. Russell reminded me that Schumann is naturally inclined anyway to throw parties in the titles for his music — *Carnavals* and *Dances of the David Club*, for goodness' sake — and he explicitly invites all his pals to be there: Chopin, Pierrot, his own alter egos Florestan and Eusebius, and every other suffering soul.

Nevertheless, this *is* a symphony, not "program music." I certainly do not believe that envisioning a party of a bunch of composers is the right or the only way to listen to the finale of the Second. But as a possible metaphor for the music's vivid gathering of composers, it seems consonant with the audible leap from symphony to song that Schumann himself hazards in this symphony. I know that I am right to take a comparable leap, and I feel Schumann in my bones when I take it. I can hear him invoking Beethoven, our common *daimon*: my loving heart reaches for what a loving heart has consecrated — *for what a loving heart has earned.*

V. TAKING CARE

In his wonderful book *Gardens: An Essay on the Human Condition*, literary scholar Robert Pogue Harrison reminds us that it was the Roman Goddess *Cura* — the lesser-known goddess of Care — whose troublesome idea it was to create humanity in the first place. We belong to *Care*, who conceived us and shaped us out the *Earth*, with the help of *Jupiter's* spirit. This is our Trinitarian nature, all three principles divine ones: Care, Earth and Heaven — but Care, in the first place. We were birthed by suffering, brought into being at suffering's hands. The point is so patently true that it must be myth to begin with.

Harrison deftly connects this pagan story of origins with the account in the book of Genesis. The expulsion of Adam and Eve from Eden, concludes Harrison, is just the right thing for them, an ironic blessing, and not merely on doctrinal grounds. They — we — take possession of our humanity, of our earthbound nature, only through being thrown out of paradise. No *theodicy* is possible here, no justification of God's ways in the face of suffering. God obviously made a mistake in entrusting Eden to a couple of boneheads. God had to learn as well as his creatures that the only way human beings can live is if they die, and the best way for us to die is to work ourselves fruitfully to death.

In helping us to understand the beauty of the Fall — a human consummation devoutly to be wished — Harrison misquotes Yeats's "Prayer to my Daughter" (the lines at the head of this chapter). Here are the original Yeats lines:

> *Hearts are not had as a gift but hearts are earned*
> *By those that are not entirely beautiful.*

The poet prays that his daughter will understand the power that intelligence and charm must wield against mere beauty, in order for a plain girl to win male hearts. He is expressing an anxious concern for his daughter's happiness in the beauty-besotted world of men.

Now, here is Harrison's misquotation:

> **Hearts are not had as gifts** *but hearts are earned*
> *By those that are not entirely beautiful.*

The error (in my added bold type) is splendid and far-reaching — a far cry from Yeats's narrow and fatherly concern. The hearts to be earned have been reflexively pluralized into our *own* hearts, nobody else's, no suitor for our own souls but ourselves. In his garden-obsessed essay, Harrison makes hay out of his misappropriation. We must cultivate, he says, the ground of our own being and dig up our own hearts. None of us is entirely beautiful and so we must each work hard at uncovering such beauty, which we will then have earned. *Take care*, intones Beethoven, warns Shakespeare, shouts McCartney, sings Schumann. *Sing your heart out. Sing so that your heart becomes one with other hearts. Then your heart will come back to you, yours at last because you gave it away.*

VI. BELOW MINIMUM WAGE

But what if you don't have the heart to sing? What if you're Jude, and all you want to say to Paul McCartney is, "F-ck off! Leave me alone! And why should I sing anyway? What the hell is there to sing about? Look around you, you stupid prat. Look at the mess we've made of things. And don't you 'hey Jude' me, 'cause, HEY, aren't *you* the one who sang about Eleanor Rigby, that poor lost sod of a soul? What about your line in there about *no one was saved*, for f-ck's sake? So don't give me all this crap about *making it better*. It's bad out there, it's cold out there, and it's going to stay that way for a very long time."

There are too many disaffected Judes like this out there. I have seen too many of them on my course rosters, shuffling late, or not at all, into my classroom. They would rather eat cut glass than sing an ode to joy. They are the undergraduate incarnations of so many antiheroes of twentieth-century music, who are well accounted for with Yiddish terminology: Arnold Schoenberg's *schlemiel* Pierrot and *schlemazel* Moses, Igor Stravinsky's *schlemazel* Oedipus and *schlemiel* Rake, Alban Berg's *nebesh* Wozzeck, Béla Bartók's *schmuck* Bluebeard, Benjamin Britten's *schmendrick* Peter Grimes, John Adams's stable of *putzes* who happen to be presidents, terrorists, and nuclear scientists. In other arenas, there's Mick Jagger doing his best to discount every gesture in life but a supremely bestial snarl, Bob Dylan, Tom Waits, and Frank Zappa screwing up their everlasting alienation in every goddamn song, rap music dissing everything in sight. Such music — from so many different arenas — fitfully embodies the *personae* of the lost ones of the world, the ones who cannot possibly earn their song, for they have not a reason to sing, nor hope, nor any possible song to sing.

The vocabulary of song has always acknowledged this spiritual predicament, a deep and ancient wisdom to be found in the technical language we have for a song's repeated figurations — *burden, strain, refrain*. Respectively, these terms express what we carry on our shoulders: *unbearable weight, untold sorrow, ritualized moderation of our grief*, all illuminating the essential difficulty of singing in the first place (and in the second and third verses, too).

The music of the past two centuries tells a monolithic, endlessly variable tale, if we can read its signs. Composers, songwriters, librettists of the twentieth century all listened very closely to the music of the nineteenth and carefully gauged its countless dramas of offering up one's voice, only in order to demonstrate how hard it is to sing at all. In music of the Romantic era, the litany of such heroic acts of *cantus interruptus* is staggering. Schubert's "Unfinished" Symphony deserves this nickname on every level of its composition. Its multiple orchestral assaults on its own sweet melodies leave them in tatters (one such outburst in the second movement is genuinely terrifying). In *Symphonie fantastique*, Berlioz sings an obsessive song of self-destructive longing, precisely and brutally so as to rip the song into shreds, along with the cruel beloved whom it represents. Chopin's most original structures are those that begin by singing and end by raging against song (the F Major Ballade beats them all). Liszt frankly does not know how to sing without interrupting the song with some ironic commentary (*une lecture*) on the tune. Mendelssohn comes closest to actually sustaining a singing voice; but he obviously and self-consciously *sets out* to transform vocal into instrumental music — an explicit "conversion" of *cantata* into *sonata* — and I've said it before, and I'll say it again: *it can't be done*. Something is always lost in translation (there is such a poignant religious subtext to this conversion for Mendelssohn). Nietzsche has said everything there is to say about how Wagner not only dismantled song in his operas, but vitiated the lyrical art altogether. This was no mere former lover's quarrel between philosopher and composer: everything about art was at stake for both of them.

This historic war waged by Romantic composers against their own singing only intensifies the miracle of Schumann's Second, with its unlikely affirmation of song.

Elsewhere in the same era, only in popular French and Italian opera did composers keep on singing with complete conviction and without irony (Nietzsche made it very clear that Bizet was his man). It is utterly without irony, too, that just about every person (read: *woman*) who possesses this capacity to sing her heart out, receives for her pains cold steel, right in the heart. Nearly every beautiful singing voice of Romantic opera dies painfully, and usually violently, in the end. Such is the fate of singing in the nineteenth century.

The composers, songwriters and librettists of the twentieth century all listened very closely to this monolithic, woeful, inexorable tale of the nineteenth. Is it any wonder, then, that their conning of this Romantic lesson (a hell of a load of home-work!) yielded a modernist Waste Land of melody gone wrong, melody gone awry, melody gone for good? After World War II, the impossibility of "earning one's song" became acute for com-posers of concert music all over the world, especially in Europe, which had suffered the greatest carnage. After enduring fascism in Germany, Italy, and France, the major German, Italian, and French composers wreaked havoc and vengeance upon those horrors by converting the musical community into a mock-fascist state, an international orthodoxy of the avant-garde. The unspoken, *unsung* dogma binding together Pierre Boulez, Karlheinz Stockhausen, Luciano Berio & Co. was the definitive dissolution of the lyrical impulse. Boulez manages it largely through color, Stockhausen through time, and Berio through parody — most ill-advisedly in his amateurish arrangements of Beatles songs — but they all manage it, as do Milton Babbitt, Elliott Carter, John Cage, & Co. in the United States.

These belated modernists remind me of the *Silent Gondoliers* of S. Morgenstern's fable. In this offbeat sequel to William Goldman's delightful *The Princess Bride*, the inscrutable S. Morgenstern tells the story of the gondoliers of Venice who go on strike, when the most skillful oarsman among them makes a mockery of the pro-fession through his awful inability to sing. As a result, every one of those whose business and particular skill it is to sing, refuses to sing, out of pure spite. With like stubbornness and perversity, the composers of the postwar avant-garde "go on strike." They could sing if they wanted to, but they refuse to do so, in pure spite over the way so many other composers are making a mockery of the profession *through their inane ability to sing*. Singing after Auschwitz is obscene; this is the implicit claim of these postwar *enfants terribles*, a corollary to Adorno's statement that "to write poetry after Auschwitz is barbaric."

Modernism reaches its peak of negative capability — and its absurd limits — with this moral outrage against song of any kind. The lyrical impoverishment of music is a willful act of asceticism,

whereby the postwar saints of modern music take upon themselves the role of the scourge, whipping music history into a
shape that justifies their own austere machinations against song.
Boulez enjoyed a specially privileged position to do this, as both
conductor and cultural arbiter on several continents. Without any
hope of earning its song, concert music of these cold, Cold-War
decades subsists below the minimum wage of musical coherence,
beneath the level of what is actually listenable, terribly proud of
itself, incapable of admitting its own arrogance, determinedly
homeless and inevitably deranged by its own hermitage. Alex
Ross tells this bizarre tale very well in his recent book, *The Rest
Is Noise*. I'm happy to have the chance to praise Ross here; his
book makes all too easy a target on other scores. I am going to
play the fox in the chicken coop in the next chapter.

The would-be loveliness of much postwar concert music
partakes of an ironic Romanticism in its audible state of lyrical fragmentation. The mangled strains of song in Boulez's
Improvisations, Babbitt's *Philomel*, Berio's heretical *Sinfonia*
— these are the destitute cousins of Schumann's ordeal in the
Second Symphony. At this later date, composers had already
been washed up on "the thither side of vital experience" (a *bon
mot* of Rebecca West), hell-bent on showing just how ridiculous
and morally bankrupt it was to sing all that stupendously ill-
conceived, Romantic stuff. *Shame on Verdi! Shame on Wagner!
Double shame on Puccini and Strauss, with all their dying heroines!
For now we know* — quoth the saints of modern music — *how
damnably hard it is to sing anything at all if we truly bear witness
to mortal pain!* Milton Babbitt's astonishingly violent sonic version of the Greek myth of *Philomel* says it all: a woman raped,
her tongue cut out by her ravisher, and then she transformed
by the gods into a nightingale, to sing her inarticulate woe for
all time. I confess, with some exhaustion, that this historical
stream of overwrought male renderings of the plight of women
— including Yeats's patronizing advice to his daughter — helped
me decide to address my final remarks in this book to my own

daughter, and to end with an appreciation of her favorite current female songwriter (Chapter 7).

"And anytime you feel the pain, hey Jude, refrain!" *No, that's all wrong, Paul, you've got it all wrong! You come so close to getting it right, but you get it wrong!* Thus yells forth in my imagination the babel of Paul McCartney's late-modernist contemporaries (some of whom actually appear on the cover of *Sgt. Pepper's Lonely Hearts Club Band*). To those unmerry men of the postwar European avant-garde, Paul McCartney's sentiment goes exactly widdershins. What composers must "refrain" from is *the refrain itself*. They must not sing. They must show how impossible it is to sing. They *must* carry the world on their shoulders. If not they, who? If not now, when? One of their dark league, the German composer Helmut Lachenmann — "laughing man" — denies his own name in absolute earnest, in works of exquisite, deliberate un-tuning, where stringed instruments can barely rise above the whispered noise the hair of their bows makes against the wood of their bodies (forget the strings; playing on the strings is almost out of the question).

Once more before I go unto the breach in the next chapter, I am glad to express my gratitude to Alex Ross for pointing out in *The Rest Is Noise* several fascinating products of the Cold-War musical era in both America and Europe, including the latter-day modernist *enfant terrible* Bernd Alois Zimmermann's massive oratorio, *Requiem for a Young Poet*, from 1969. *Mirabile dictu,* Zimmermann presents fragments from both Beethoven's Ninth and the (then newly minted) "Hey Jude," both brutally drowned out by the harshly declaiming voices of Stalin, Goebbels, and Churchill. With brutal, self-lacerating *Schadenfreude,* Zimmermann — "room man" — drops his incendiary bombs onto the rooms that used to house song. History overwhelms song. Period. End of story. What's far worse, history overwhelms *our particular songs,* Beethoven's and the Beatles', the very ones we have invoked in order to demonstrate the feasibility of earning our songs.

Do I disagree with Zimmermann's grievous assessment?
No.
Will I surrender to it?
Not on your life.

VII. ALL HALLOWS

In 1997, I composed an overture for large orchestra called *All Hallows*, inspired by a short story of the same name by the twentieth-century English author, Walter de la Mare. In this weird tale, a visitor to a remote and ancient church is shown evidence of hideous repairs wrought upon the building's masonry by invisible — and presumably demonic — hands. The key question posed by the puzzled pilgrim is this: *Why would demons build something up only for the purpose of destroying it in the end?* This same question might serve as a syllabus for the study of the twentieth century.

The story's most gripping passage recounts a confrontation with the fearful presences at work in the church. For the narrator, it is a very close call. The thrill of de la Mare's narrative springs from the same source as all great tales of the supernatural: they provide a strangely cheering way to address the proximity of evil, the need of every human being to confront it, and the giddy hope that it will pass by.

At some point in composing the piece, I discovered that a familiar *cantus firmus* of Western music — a snippet of Gregorian chant on which apprentice composers over many generations had built their craft — possessed the very same contour as a phrase of Jewish hymnody, *Ani Ma'amim*, chanted (according to witnesses) by groups of victims on their way to the gas chambers at Auschwitz. The accord between these two melodies — the one an audible sign of musical art, the other a devastating, almost obscene, emblem of Jewish faith — struck me as a dark revelation, simple enough to be profound.

Halfway through my overture, de la Mare's demons come into view, very close indeed, clanging a vast battery of percussion, which my percussionist friend Chris — who played one of the parts at the premiere — still jokes about. The original story makes no bones about the impossibility of doing anything to ward off this *danse macabre*. The narrator just has to sit it out. I decided that my music could not be so inert. After its near-collision with the demon-army of construction workers, the orchestra collapses into a post-traumatic hush (a far cry from Schumann's anticipatory hush) and then gradually gathers itself to sing the death-camp hymn *Ani Ma'amim*. After Auschwitz, there can be no mere hymnody. The tune is compelled to deliver both its own faithful lyric

> *And even though the Messiah tarries*
> *— even so, I believe in his coming*

and, at the same time, something on the order of the obscene title of Tadeusz Borowski's novel about Auschwitz:

> *This way for the gas, ladies and gentlemen*

and the music swells to a second crisis that is even more demon-laden than the first, in its utter helplessness and hopelessness.

At this point, my overture is properly poised to admit defeat, naturally inclined to plummet down into the musical avant-garde's moral high ground of lyrical asceticism, of absolute renunciation of song. But there is another way. *There is always another way.* The little *cantus firmus* — the "firm song" — rises out of this nowhere of un-song, strangely echoing the song of the murdered ones, but following its own luminous course, as if nothing had happened, as if everything were happening now. At first, the *cantus* is shouted down by the scandalized brass, but it starts up again, ready for anything . . . except for what happens. As the bassoons sing the *cantus firmus* over and over again, the conductor turns around on the podium and starts singing the *cantus firmus* himself, while conducting the audience to begin singing it along with him. Everybody in the whole damn concert hall sings the *cantus firmus*, nowhere left in the hall not to sing, a *plenum* of singing. Even the sorry-ass Judes in the hall sing, shocked into singing by a conductor on a podium waving his arms at them to raise their sorry-ass voices out of their disaffected silence.

My friend Kenneth Schermerhorn, the conductor of the Nashville Symphony, commissioned *All Hallows* and led its premiere. When he first saw my directions in the score for this climactic passage of audience singing, he called me on the phone and said, with real panic in his voice, "Michael, my dear, it won't work. Please don't ask me to do this. You will make fools of us both." I reminded him what he had told me some years earlier, after having heard scenes of my bad first opera performed in workshop. He said, "Michael, my dear, the problem with your opera is that it is too *nice*. You are not taking the music enough by the balls." When he heard me quote these words of his back at him, he stopped trying to talk me out of it and told me instead to pray for us both.

On the night of its premiere — Halloween, 1997, All Hallows' Eve — there were 2,500 people in the hall. They were not there to hear my overture, but to hear the aged Isaac Stern try to pull off one more performance of Bruch. But they were *there*, nonetheless. Two and a half thousand people sang my *cantus firmus* when Kenneth turned around and conducted them to. I am not imagining this. I was there. Everybody in the hall was singing. When I met him backstage, Mr. Stern said to me, in his inimitable growl, "So you're the guy who has the audience singing. You and Lenny Bernstein. Well, somebody's got to do it."

As Kenneth kept the audience singing the *cantus firmus* — do re fa mi la sol fa mi re do — he also drew the orchestra back into play, different instruments entering with different counterpoints against the audience's ongoing song. I engineered this passage as a gleeful parody of Mozart's "Jupiter" finale, which is itself a gleeful parody of antique counterpoint, spoofing the very same *cantus firmus*.

What species of counterpoint arrives in the orchestra, to sing in cahoots with the audience? Who comes to *my* "war party" in the last couple minutes of *All Hallows*, banding together to wage tuneful battle against the demons? Who are the angelic *daimones* I summon to exorcise their dark brother-demons from the sanctuary of song? Who are these presences, whose aid I require to reverse Zimmermann's incendiary attack, fight fire with fire, shout all the demons of history back down into Orcus where there is no song? I make my overture to these heroes, enlisting their help to cast the demons back down below the musical ground of my *cantus firmus*, Mozart's *cantus firmus*, every implausibly hopeful composer's *cantus firmus*.

Mahler comes first, his invocation to the Creator Spirit rising in the trombones; then comes Bach, a fragment of a sweet prelude; then the kiss for all the world from Beethoven's Ninth; then Schumann's vision of Beethoven in his Second; then the great song from the Finale of Brahms's First, which is a gloss on both Beethoven and Schumann; then Paul's "Hey Jude," right alongside a phrase from *Rodeo*, which first unleashed in me the chutzpah to be what I wanted to be, just as Copland — a Jewish boy from Brooklyn — deftly rode the great horns of his American dilemma.

In his *Requiem*, Bernd Alois Zimmerman invokes Beethoven and the Beatles in order to crush them under the demons of the twentieth century. I invoke the exact same tunes — and all their beautiful company — in order to crush the demons. Which of us is right? Which of us is wrong? *No! There is no "right" or "wrong." There is only human suffering and the possibility of combating it. There are only allies and enemies in this struggle.* Under this overarching dispensation, it is likely that if I had known of Zimmermann's piece back in 1997, I would have had him at my Halloween party, too.

In *Black Lamb and Grey Falcon*, Rebecca West writes, "All our Western thought is founded on this repulsive pretence, that pain is the proper price of any good thing." She makes this observation in the course of her brilliant peroration against our founding religions, which originally called for the slaughter of innocents as a sacrifice — whether it is the Old Testament animal offerings or the New Testament Crucifixion. In the end, I am as guilty of West's Western pathology as anyone else. In the last minute of *All Hallows*, Amadeus Mozart arrives with his peerless help against the demons, ready and eager to pound out his jovial version of our common *cantus firmus* from the finale of the "Jupiter." But I will not let him do it. Through a perverse kenosis that remains inscrutable to me at this distance of 13 years, my violins deliver Mozart's rejoicing motto with the stuffing knocked out of it, at a dark and almost inaudible *pianissimo*, immediately drowned out by a sudden retaliation of the demons, my friend Chris ushering them back into view with an instrument actually called a "lion's roar." The overture ends with one final stroke of the demonic anvil, the demons dead set again on their horrible work.

I sent a recording of this premiere performance of *All Hallows* to my mentor, the composer Samuel Adler, a refugee from the Nazis at the age of nine. A few days later, Sam called me on the phone and proceeded to yell at me for half an hour for my cowardice, my betrayal, my surrender to evil, my failure of nerve to uphold the goodness I had set in motion, my capitulation to darkness, my unforgivable drowning out of Mozart. He really blasted me. He said, "How dare you end such a glorious celebration on such a note of defeat? How dare you play a coward's part? Michael, you had a chance to write perhaps the great ethical testament of our time, and you blew it. I was there, in Mannheim, and the SS guards almost took me and my father. You think I don't know what it means to be afraid of demons? You have the luxury, the aesthetic pretence of imagining evil's triumph. Shame on you."

What could I say? He was right. But I knew I was also right to give the demons the last word — the last clangor. In the first place, that's what de la Mare's story demanded. But there was more to it than mere fidelity to my literary source. My imagining evil's triumph was no "aesthetic pretence," but rather an acknowledgment of the insanity Rebecca West identifies. I cannot be Mozart, who (as West herself remarks with awe) could never write a single note that was not agreeable. I am much closer to West herself in spirit and practice: in order to argue for what is agreeable, I feel the compulsion to spend a good portion of my energy providing an unflinching inventory of what is disagreeable. Mozart is one of the very few who managed the conclusive victory of the agreeable over the disagreeable. For the radical children of modernism in our time, the only thing left for a composer to do is to serve as curators of the conclusive victory of the disagreeable over the agreeable. I am productively discontent walking the narrow bridge between these two positions, the only place I feel at home.

Chapter 4

The Rest of *The Rest Is Noise*

Alex Ross's bestselling book deserves all the accolades it has received. It is the most readable account of twentieth-century music since Gerald Abraham's magnificent *A Hundred Years of Music*, which could only go so far in its final edition of 1964. Ross's book is the required text in my "Modernism and Music" freshman seminar at Vanderbilt, a perfect read for eighteen-year-olds, most of whom have never even thought about modern music before. It turns music history into a human story; that is, the book implicitly makes the case that the only way in which history can be meaningful is when we can *dramatize* it. The complex web of personalities and ideas running through twentieth-century music is adroitly subsumed by Ross as the pretext for his largely political narrative, which — like his weekly *New Yorker* reviews — is a pleasure to read, artfully surpassing any actual pleasure we might glean from listening to some of the more difficult music he writes about every week. Right from its Shakespearean parody of a title, *The Rest Is Noise* is an artwork unto itself, a sort of music in prose. Moreover, the story Ross tells has an ethical edge, restoring from obscurity to the bright light of Ross's intelligence both personages and predicaments warranting our serious attention, if we are to grasp as a whole the past century's music in the context of its relentless tragedy.

I highly recommend the book. But I cannot love it. I have searched my feelings for any taint of jealousy over Ross's literary success, but that's not the problem. I am a composer who enjoys writing and strives to write well, nothing more or less. The problem is that I expect too much from Ross. For years, I panted desperately for a text I could share with my freshmen, something they could carry with them as a worthy companion to their courageous investigations of modernist music. I really had hoped that Ross's would be the one, and now it is, by default. Therefore, the book's flaws are heartbreaking to me and a source of confusion and misery in the class.

In sum, there are four basic problems *The Rest Is Noise* cannot solve, since Ross has willfully embraced them as virtues:

1) The book's narrative impulse is to lift up so many massive, competing "trees" (Berlin in the Twenties, Stalin's Russia) that there can be no possibility of a "forest ecology." In short, Ross loses his forest through his trees. Scheherazade-like, he blithely tells one rich tale after another, without any desire to weave them into a single fabric. But such an overall narrative pattern for twentieth-century music is not only possible to project, it is *obligatory* for such a tangled web of historical forces — as long as the pattern remains supple and subject to change, like any good hypothesis. Ross leaves us thrilled, overwhelmed, dazzled by his storytelling, but bereft of any hope of understanding the ties that bind the century together (how tight those bonds are, how they draw blood!). The problem is exacerbated all the more when certain key composers — Strauss, Schoenberg, Shostakovich, a conspiracy of S's — keep popping up like bad pfennigs (or rotten rubles) from chapter to chapter, keeping Ross's story consistent, and anachronistically

"heroic" — as if the Romantic interest of his novelistic account trumps everything else, including many silenced composers.

2) Because of the narrative self-sufficiency of each chapter (music under the Nazis, music during the Cold War), the book can have no genuine *synchronic* sensibility. The genius of the twentieth century resides in the unprecedented presence of radically disparate voices at the same moment. Such voices are to be found in the book, but their "dissonant" simultaneity is lost in the shuffle. This failure of the book to uphold, in true counterpoint, the century's *synchronic diversity of sound and resources* has the air of a broken promise, especially after Ross pays immediate lip service to this defining feature of the century's music on the first page of his Preface, with an anecdote about a meeting between George Gershwin and Alban Berg. Literally and philosophically, these two great contemporaries — with their wonderful spectrographic extremes of harmonic color — never meet again for the rest of the book.

3) *The Rest Is Noise* expresses incredible contempt (i.e., neglect) for important and beautiful music that clearly has no narrative, political, or ethical purchase for Ross. It is unaccountable for a book about twentieth-century music — especially because it promises to be representative rather than comprehensive — to lavish dozens of pages of attention on Richard Strauss (a child of the nineteenth) and a meager ten pages *in toto* on Béla Bartók, who, for many composers and music lovers, serves — against so many odds — as the spiritual and ethical conscience of the epoch. Others fare even worse in Ross's hands. In his published review of *The Rest Is Noise*, the contemporary English composer David Matthews has smartly slapped Ross on the wrist for ignoring Ralph Vaughan Williams and Carl Nielsen (the finest symphonists alongside Shostakovich) and, even worse (because more in need of attention on

this side of the Atlantic), Sir Michael Tippett, the only composer who deserves, along with Olivier Messiaen, the epithet of a true visionary in his generation. These things are not matters of taste, but serious flaws in a book purporting to steer clear of aesthetic stinginess and exclusiveness. I am thankful to Ross at least for rescuing Sibelius' name from its ignoble expropriation by a music software product. It is all the more shocking, therefore, that in one fatal sentence, Ross gleans a whole crop of English composers, including Vaughan Williams, tossing them — along with Bartók — into a shallow ditch he calls "folkish." Ross has created the illusion of giving us a more generous survey of the century's musical ordnance, but when he passes over the Eastern European and English countryside of Bartók and Vaughan Williams without observing more than one or two significant landmarks, the unreliable scale of Ross's survey becomes obvious.

4) Like all good telescopes, *The Rest Is Noise* narrows vertiginously at the end through which it looks. Ross gives us a hasty "Music at Century's End," as depressing a laundry list as could be found in any undergraduate textbook. It is all the more dispiriting because the writing is so *good*, and therefore gives an illusion of sufficiency, when it ought to beat its breast for the sin of making such a brief and tidy counting of rosary beads for recently passed and still-living composers.

All right, that's enough. I'm done griping. Now let's get back to musical ground and attack these problems one by one, offering at least the beginnings of a solution to each one.

*First question: how to propose a **narrative pattern** for the music of the twentieth century? How to offer up **a forest ecology**, when there are so many different species and sizes of tree, bound up with so much inextricable cultural "undergrowth"? It is impossible to* *reduce this manifold history to a single idea, and there is no danger of that here. In the preceding chapter, I've already presented an idea about the evolution of music in the twentieth century — the increasing difficulty of earning one's song — different from the one I will now propose. My paradoxical point is that a good, plausible, single, generous, overarching idea (any idea, rather than no idea, which is Ross's fault) can help to enlarge the complexity of much that transpired along one extraordinary line of musical inquiry — in this case, an idea that constituted one of the rare and synchronous breakthroughs of the human spirit.*

I have adapted the nutshell of a text which follows from an essay I wrote some years ago for concertgoers at my school of music, to help them make connections among the diverse programs of a twentieth-century retrospective. This essay-within-an-essay traces concert music from the springs of modernism in the late nineteenth century to the end of World War II. In it, you will find composers and pieces that are treated at much greater length by Alex Ross. My goal is to replace his discrete narratives of the modernist mainstream with a single, conceptual one — a peg on which to hang the "aesthetic overcoat" of the twentieth century. Music is not the same as ideas; but every piece of music contains both sound and idea.

I. OF BARE FEET AND BARED SOULS: MODERNIST MUSIC, 1888–1945

In 1888, a dapper young Frenchman named Erik Satie re-invented music. From the Greek, he coined the name *Gymnopédies* — "dances of naked boys" — for three lovely, miniature piano pieces in stately measure, music such as the figures on Keats's urn might be dancing to. Number one of the set sounds so familiar to us from various commercial adaptations that we no longer have any clue how strange it is, much less how utterly alien it was from anything else appearing in 1888.

There is nothing very ambitious about the *Gymnopédies*; but the spirit in which they are written is epoch-making. Like the musical innovators of Florence who created opera 300 years before him, Satie forges the new by re-imagining the archaic. His leap of historical imagination becomes a source of inspiration for the Egyptian art of Picasso, the Homeric texts of Joyce and Pound, and the pagan scenarios of Debussy, Ravel, and Stravinsky.

Satie "re-invents" music in the literal sense: not finding what he needs in the seething Romantic stew surrounding him, he starts from scratch. If one thing in general can be said about the key figures of twentieth-century art, music, and literature, it is that *they start from scratch*. They seek first causes and first principles, dig down to the roots and raw materials of how their work comes into being in the first place. Sublimely scornful of prevailing tradition or public taste, Satie sets a luminous and thrilling example for the age of modernism by rejecting the weight of accumulated culture, jettisoning everything that does not belong to his own idiosyncratic imagination, going buck naked during an age of costly attire: not merely *gymnopodie* (barefoot), but *gymnopedie* (bare-bottomed). It is no wonder he was a hero to generations of avant-garde composers and artists, however modest his actual musical achievement may have been.

In order to reject a tradition in good faith, you must first try it on. It is impossible for an artist to approach the drawing board empty-handed (or empty-headed), completely free of the burden of any responsibility to tradition. The great composers of the twentieth century begin their careers fully freighted with historical baggage. Arnold Schoenberg and Igor Stravinsky, the two musical giants of our century, start off as the perfect avatars of old-fashioned compositional practice. In his early masterpiece, *Transfigured Night* of 1899, Schoenberg shoulders, Atlas-like, the whole world of lush Wagnerian harmony, going further with it than anyone before or since. In his debut ballet score of 1910, *The Firebird*, Stravinsky takes Romantic nationalism to its sensual limit, beating his mentor Rimsky-Korsakov at the old man's great Russian game. Schoenberg and Stravinsky — along with Claude Debussy, Richard Strauss, and others — worked together to close the frontier of musical Romanticism, staking its final claims. Once that adventure was finished, there was no quenching their pioneer spirit: a new frontier must be opened.

In every age, music draws from what's going on in the other arts. Such cross-currents rise to flood level in early twenti-eth-century Europe. Creators in all fields of artistic endeavor — literature, theatre, the visual arts, architecture, music, and dance — now take their bearings from each other, turning the culture into a dizzying network of interrelations. Artists also begin to take direct cues from science, technology, politics and psychology. The frontier of modernism buzzes with these fruitful cross-pollinations. Debussy discovers the blueprints for his new edifices of sound in the language of French Symbolist poetry, with its elusive suggestions, its withholding of conclusive meanings and its exaltation of sound over sense. Without the poet Stéphane Mallarmé (author of "The Afternoon of a Faun"), there would be no musical Impressionism. Consider, too, the pair of friends who share the name Claude: the seductive assaults on harmony in Debussy is of a piece with the gorgeous tactics against figuration in Monet.

The alliance of so many writers, artists and musicians towards the overturning of tradition is unprecedented in the history of the arts. For the creators themselves, the goal was practically the same: to get to the bottom of experience by getting to the bottom of art — to the actual sounds words make, the way light hits the brush stroke on the flat canvas, the sonority of the isolated chord or flute tone. This great coincidence for the modernists between the physical and spiritual dimensions of art has permanently col-ored the way we now understand language, vision, and sound.

The German art scene at century's open, if compared to the French, seems like the dark side of the moon. Richard Strauss's overheated *Salome* of 1905 — the temperature rises even higher in his *Elektra* of three years later — delivers a disturbing message taken up by other artists as a kind of manifesto: *the line between beauty and terror is very thin* (see Chapter 5). Given Strauss's retreat into operatic nostalgia in years to come, he patently has no intention in 1905 of carrying a torch for the avant-garde. He wants nothing more than to be a showman, an operatic illusionist of the first order. But his wedding of ecstasy and disgust in those two early sensational operas — Salome kissing John the Baptist's severed head, all glorious hell breaking loose in the orchestra — exerts an enduring fascination for composers of the time. Both Alex Ross in his book and the superb historian Barbara Tuchman (in *The Proud Tower*) make much of Strauss's nearly clinical portrayals of madness as the audible signs of Europe's decadence. Meanwhile, to Strauss himself, it was all a fantastic lark: he insisted to his orchestra players at the first rehearsal of *Elektra* that it should sound like Mendelssohn's *A Midsummer Night's Dream*.

Arnold Schoenberg later wrote that he was glad he did not recognize the "P. T. Barnum side" of Richard Strauss. For Schoenberg, Strauss's operatic achievement in the early years of the twentieth century is not merely a theatrical coup, but an invitation to a higher calling, a spur to artistic risk-taking of a deeply moral purpose. Schoenberg feels empowered by *Salome* and *Elektra* to go the distance in a dark journey of the soul — a journey that was, for him, not a matter of choice but of necessity, inexorably dragging him out of the complacent waters of the nineteenth century and into the raging sea of the anxious present.

Beauty and terror, ecstasy and disgust — these are the polarities that Schoenberg and other German expressionists mold into unities, and they confront the listener with indissoluble difficulty in Schoenberg's atonal works. Nearly a century has passed since its first performance in Vienna, but still *Pierrot Lunaire* (for actress and chamber ensemble) will not yield up the secret of its paradoxes. In this music, the most opaque lunacy is shot through with a bright light of musical invention; an abject terror of life is illuminated by a confident vision of what life is like now, and how it must be contended with. It is a vision that expresses, with uncanny artistic control, the perilous condition of derangement. Pierrot — the centuries-old clown of *commedia dell'arte* — now becomes capable of atrocities of the imagination. In love with the unreachable and antic moon, he metamorphoses into the twentieth-century composer.

Listeners continue to ask in bewilderment, why does Schoenberg submit himself and his audience to such ravages of harmony, such distortions of song, such inscrutable images of madness and horror? This surely, is not what music was meant for; this is not the way things ought to be. Audiences who are struck in this fashion with fear and loathing for *Pierrot Lunaire*, in fact understand it perfectly. Indeed, many come to love and admire the work for this reason. Schoenberg looks at the world around him, at its institutions, its frenzied pace, its mangled aspirations. Then he looks into his own heart: there is no correspondence between them, no harmony, no common ground — only confusion and alienation. By 1912, modern life has outrun the human soul. Two years later, the distance and the dissonance between them would collapse into the worst nightmare of war the world has ever suffered. In *Pierrot* and other beautifully disorienting works, Schoenberg takes the pulse of a culture that is veering precipitously towards ripping the heart from its own chest (as Pierrot does midway through the song cycle).

To call Schoenberg's atonal compositions "beautiful" is an ethical matter as well as an aesthetic one. The listener to his music, like the viewer of Beckmann's paintings or Giacometti's statues, or the reader of Kafka's fables, discovers that the artist's courage to name unspeakable anxiety and to catalogue immeasurable dread is bound up with an ability to articulate *from scratch* what harmony consists of, and in what ways modernity has disavowed it. These masters of the irrational are great by virtue of their lucidity. There can be no greater paradox than that, and no greater blessing to those who wish sincerely to be accountable to a century of unparalleled cruelty, inhumanity and slaughter.

Gustav Mahler, Schoenberg's mentor and supporter in Vienna — and fellow Jew in a city where to be Jewish was to be a problematic outsider — stands somewhat anterior to our discussion, for he sounds the glorious death knell of an older century. But we can at least include his encounter with another Jewish Viennese luminary, Dr. Sigmund Freud. As the story goes, Freud diagnosed Mahler as suffering from "an emotional maladjustment due to a childhood trauma." There being no escape from Freudian psychologizing in our time — it may be the century's signature — we might as well embrace the diagnosis as a peculiarly apt one for the twentieth century itself, and for its art in particular.

The century's pre-trauma "childhood" comprises the years leading up to 1914, during which artists, full of uninhibited and childlike wonder, burst forth with new paradigms for music, the visual arts and literature. Cubism, justly the most famous of these paradigm shifts, comes down to us from a Paris of almost incredible splendor and artistic resources, as a peculiar embodiment of modernist *joie de vivre*. From 1909 to 1913, the cubist canvases and collages of Picasso and Braque evolve through a series of astonishing developments — a lifetime of discovery concentrated into five years. At the same time and in the same city, Stravinsky composes three ballets that offer us, in a bewildering nutshell, the essence of twentieth-century music. The nexus between Stravinsky and Picasso is one of the wonders of twentieth-century art: in the half-hour of music and dance that is *The Rite of Spring*, the spirit of cubism triumphs beyond any recall, marking a point of no return for the imagination of artists and musicians to come.

Even the act of writing about these matters turns naturally towards an experiment in cubist technique. In the paragraph that follows, painting and music should be imagined simultaneously. Let's see how it works:

[*The Rite*]   [flow of music]
The effect of cubist art is literally shattering: the observable world

                                    [melodic fragment]
splinters into a thousand pieces, each shard   belonging

    [harmonic context]   [rhythmic frame]
to a spatial plane   or moment of time distinct from the rest.

                        [blocks of sound]
The cubist breakdown of objects   into multi-layered

[polychords and polyrhythms]
geometric components   is certainly a destructive act,

                                [harmony and rhythm]
specifically in its explosion of traditional representation

    [music]
in painting. But out of the debris rises a new universe of

                    [aural]
possibilities, in which the visual image is no longer bound by a

    [meter]   [predictable rhythmic pattern]
single perspective, nor caught in frozen time.

                    [sound]
As never before, the image comes alive with restless motion and

                                [ears]
disorienting energy, dancing before the eyes as a revelation of

    [music]   [common tonal practice]
what painting has always been behind its figurative illusionism:

[phrases, timbres, chords, metric regularities]
shapes, colors, planes, time captured.   But not until now,

[Igor Stravinsky]   **[music]**
Picasso and Braque show us, have artists been able to set painting

free into the irreducible multiplicity of ephemeral experience

. . . into shifting space and rapidly passing time.

Shifting space and rapidly passing time — these coordinates
become the abiding state of mind for every citizen of a techno-
logically-transformed century. The automobile, the telephone,
the wireless and the airplane effectively dislodge people from
their fixtures of set place and nature-based time. The Eiffel
Tower (a favorite subject of modernist painters) stands as the
quintessential artifact of the age because, apart from its aesthetic
magnificence, it is a functional radio tower, the first of its size
and transmission capacity. (Stephen Kern's book, *The Culture of
Time and Space*, treats the dizzying "space-time continuum" of
modernism with breathtaking synchronicity.)

In this whirlwind of change, the "children" of the early twentieth-century art grow up together, risking their necks in games
no one has ever played before, driven to limn the world along
unprecedented lines. Later in this chapter, we will test the limits
of this modernist *Zeitgeist* and "lay the ghost," which still spooks
its artistic offspring even now, a century later.

In *The Rite of Spring*, Stravinsky goes back to the childhood
of humanity itself. On opening night in 1913, Nijinsky's gro-
tesquely primitive choreography — even more than Stravinsky's
wild music — held up a savage mirror to its refined twentieth-
century audience. The jolt of recognition was so scandalous, so
revolting, that the mild "incident" previously organized by an
anti-Stravinsky cabal erupted into a full-fledged riot.

At the end of *The Rite*, the chosen virgin dances herself to
death. A year after its premier, the enormity of an entire civilization sacrificing itself to the gods of nationalism and greed
comes like a demoniac distortion of Stravinsky's vision. With its
millions of dead and its corruption of technology in the service

of wholesale slaughter, the Great War of 1914–19 traumatically ends the century's childhood.

In the aftermath of war, "starting from scratch" has a new and poignant ring to it for the history of music. Many European composers devise a consistent strategy to get past the all-too-real catastrophe of the Great War and re-establish their imaginative lives. Continuing our "case study" of the twentieth century, we can put in psychoanalytical terms: the *enfants terribles* of modernism regress, after their trauma, into rational worlds of elaborate control and ultimate order.

For Stravinsky, this regression takes the form of *neoclassicism*: a series of re-creations — or "masques" — of more or less distant musical pasts, each one serving as a spiritual refuge on account of its wholeness, its otherness, its *pastness*. Yet again, the parallels to Picasso's art of the same interwar period are wonderful. In *Pulcinella*, Stravinsky puts on the comic mask of eighteenth-century Italian music; in *Oedipus Rex*, it is the tragic mask of ancient Greece; in *The Symphony of Psalms*, he puts on the otherworldly skullcap of Hebrew scripture, distanced yet further by translation into medieval Latin, distanced yet further by his own Russian Orthodoxy. These works, technically dazzling and aesthetically puzzling, are both utopian in their appropriations of the past, and dystopian in the composer's "unfocusing" of the past through his own uncompromisingly modern ear.

Schoenberg's regressive path leads into music that would be good accompaniment to Hermann Hesse's novel, *Magister Ludi*, in which a monastic order keeps the flame of post-apocalyptic culture alive by means of a "glass-bead game" of exceeding complexity. Schoenberg's twelve-tone music is the glass-bead game of the twentieth century, a strange mixture of artistic hopefulness and desperation. His dodecaphony harnesses the irrational impulses of *Pierrot Lunaire* into mathematical matrices. Works like the Piano Suite and Variations for Orchestra also breathe an air of neoclassicism, molding past forms into new shapes, while drawing strength from their bygone stability.

Schoenberg's student Anton Webern becomes the real *magister* of the twelve-tone game. He conducts research into utterances of profoundest brevity, where isolated tones pulse like a telegraphy of the soul. Webern's music will assume a scriptural aura at mid-century; for many composers, it draws the logical outcomes of music's phenomenological "starting from scratch."

Another compositional strategy between the wars takes a less cerebral form. Instead of retreating into other worlds, certain composers embrace the world as they find it, especially the domain of popular music. Jazz and dance-hall tunes of the 1920s convey a feeling of frenetic joy and abandon, qualities that must have acted in compensation for the death-grip of the war years. Concert composers soak up this energy like schoolboys at recess, starved for tactile experience (a number of them were just that). Darius Milhaud's *Le Creation du monde* pulls together Harlem jazz and classical chamber music (Gershwin's *Rhapsody in Blue* would do the same a couple years later) into a hybrid ballet that presumes to make a fresh start, right from the creation of the world (as African-American folktales envision it). Milhaud's companions in the group of French composers called *Les Six* all compose in one popular dialect or another. Listening to Francis Poulenc's songs, it's hard not to light up a cigarette and drink a shot of absinthe.

All this time in Connecticut, Charles Ives operates like a one-man patent office, inventing — as this or that technique suits his eccentric purpose — bitonality, atonality, post-tonality, polychords, polyrhythms, "cubist" simultaneity and collage, and every manner of adaptation of folk and popular music, in some cases coming up with the stuff years before any of it happened across the pond. Stravinsky and Schoenberg come to acknowledge Ives's place alongside them; but Ives has more local fish to fry — some of them leaping right out of Walden pond. The "scratch" Ives starts from is at one with Emerson's and Thoreau's: a *tabula rasa* laid by Nature hard by and ascending into the Universe, not one of its questions answered.

Like Ives, Béla Bartók stands at some geographic and spiritual distance from the European modernist mainstream (and from Alex Ross's attention). I will have more to say later in this chapter about Bartók's ways of opposing the depredations of the twentieth century. The crucial point is his *ethical* stance: Bartók makes a defiant music, holding fast to truths terribly embattled not only by war, but by modernity itself. He embarks on a far-flung mission to preserve the rural folkways of Hungarians and southern Slavs, traveling from one village to another with a wax-cylinder phonograph, in some cases inventing from scratch new kinds of music notation to account for various folks' strange musical practices. Bartók's wedding of peasant dance and avant-garde experimentation in his six string quartets is the century's *cri de coeur*: how can we move forward and not leave all we hold dear behind? Bartók is one composer who finds a way.

It is a marvel that more of these composers do not despair when they find themselves working for a civilization that builds itself up only to destroy itself in the end (like de la Mare's demons). In one extraordinary instance, a pit of despair furnishes a composer with the unclean slate he needs to create a radiant vision of transcendence: Olivier Messiaen writes his *Quartet for the End of Time* in 1941, for both his fellow inmates and his German captors in a POW camp.

With a good deal less affirmation, the Soviet composer Dmitri Shostakovich makes despair into his life's work. His courage and subterfuge in confronting the most murderous tyranny humanity has ever known (under Stalin) are matched only by the danger and terror he submitted himself to in the process. The harrowing circumstances of his Fifth Symphony — well narrated by Alex Ross — show just how close he comes to losing his life (as untold numbers of his fellow Soviet artists actually did), and how closer even than that he comes to losing his soul. Shostakovich's various odes to Stalin are passports to music's lowest circles of hell, racing down the steep slope right alongside the music of the murdered composers of Theresienstadt. These unbearable testimonies — the one celebrating evil, the other perishing from it — scratch at the bare feet of the twentieth century until they stream with innocent blood.

This last, distressing image gives an indispensable twist to my organizing idea of twentieth-century music's *starting from scratch*. Ross is preoccupied for many pages with Shostakovich because the composer is blown so hard by the winds of the century's political nightmares. From start to finish, *The Rest Is Noise* identifies the unsavory work of musical politics with forensic aplomb, "listening to the twentieth century" (the book's subtitle) far more attentively than to its actual music. On a different tack — listening to the composers themselves — I end my own tour of the modernist era with Shostakovich because his tortured music puts a period — a shrieking exclamation point — to the *musical* principle that nourished so many composers before the politicians and mass murderers got their bloody hands on it. These composers and their artist-allies hoped to start from scratch, but most of them (apart from the war-maddened Italian *futuristi*) could not imagine what shape the very same spirit of cultural clearance would take in the hands of Hitler, Stalin, and Mussolini.

Robert Pogue Harrison, whose fine misquotation of Yeats I cited in Chapter 3, deserves to be quoted accurately and at length on this matter, again from his book on *Gardens*:

> Crucial to modernism was the attack, the assault, and the occasion to propagate cultural violence in the name of spiritual liberation . . .. The risk of an aggravated cultural militancy is that it partakes of, or employs, the same forces of disfiguration it presumes to counteract. To a certain degree this was unavoidable. After all, our destructive and creative powers arise from the same basic source. The vandal's hammer is the same as the sculptor's . . .. Destruction can be liberating, inebriating, creative, and even beautiful; and certainly clearing the ground is a precondition for the productive

work of cultivation. Yet much of what we call modernism, in its militant activism, did not take the next step: it did not commit itself to the work of cultivation . . . the painstaking, compensatory work of fostering the saving power of human culture. As a result, modernism found its objective correlative [T. S. Eliot's term for a poem's sign of its own essential feeling] in the wasteland rather than the garden.

Harrison gives us the disturbing hook we need to understand both modernist music itself and the monstrous century in which it flourished. But modernism is just one thread of the twentieth-century musical fabric. The work of interweaving must now begin.

Second question: how to be true to the enormous stylistic dispari-ties at work in the music in the twentieth century? How to celebrate widely opposing composers and their achievements as synchronous products of the complex chemistry we call history, rather than as separable distillates of this or that particular historical experi-ment (which is the strategy of Ross's narrative alembic)? How not to grind the axe of a zeitgeist, but rather to brauchen Zeit — *to take time, to avail oneself of time, to bind up time's wounds after so many foolish, academic battles to claim one sort of history as the only rightful accounting of time? Alex Ross wisely begins his book with the story of how Berg and Gershwin met, and how Berg told Gershwin, "Music is music." Now let us see how Ross's wisdom — and Berg's — may unfold in ways that the rest of* The Rest Is Noise *remains strangely silent on. Ross pats Gershwin on the back appropriately and heartily throughout his book; therefore, I think it's only fair to play instead a tuneful dark horse against Gershwin, someone Ross has neither the zeit nor the geist for — no one darker, no one looking more like a horse (oh, those hands' breadth!) than Sergei Rachmaninoff.*

II. LAYING THE ZEITGEIST

During a 12-month period in 1934–35, two very different musical works came into being: Alban Berg's *Violin Concerto* and
Sergei Rachmaninoff's *Rhapsody on a Theme of Paganini*. Both
are acknowledged masterpieces, both welcomed by large symphonic audiences. The pair of works represent a typical moment
in the twentieth century's musical history when two styles of
vastly disparate technical means and aesthetic ends coexisted,
albeit uncomfortably, and produced, in both cases, music of the
first excellence. The two pieces constitute the most extensive
exploration yet of their respective creative landscapes, with
landmark after unmistakable landmark from previous works
charted out now with yet more daring and *éclat*.

Perhaps the fact that they are concertos has something to do
with this new level of virtuosity. But the medium of soloist and
orchestra does not by itself explain the extraordinary success of
these works. The genre was not a sure-fire winner for Berg and
Rachmaninoff: the former's *Chamber Concerto* of 1925 and the
latter's *Fourth Piano Concerto* of 1926 do not rank among their
finest creations. Moreover, the concerto was not the genre closest
to their hearts. Berg considered himself an opera composer first
and foremost. The commission of the *Violin Concerto* interrupted
the massive enterprise of *Lulu*, which remained unfinished at his
death that same year. Dead before his new concerto's first performance, Berg was not around to see it quickly become one of
the most performed and beloved works of the twentieth-century
violin repertoire. Meanwhile, Rachmaninoff toiled to make his
mark as a pure symphonist. He longed to escape from his reputa-
tion as a piano virtuoso, whereby he traveled around the world
performing as soloist, usually in his first three piano concertos.
(This aspect of his career was at its peak in 1934). The *Rhapsody
of a Theme of Paganini* was, above all, a means for Rachmaninoff
the pianist to offset the sheer boredom of his own concerto repertoire. More fortunate than Berg in both audience and longevity,

Rachmaninoff enjoyed for many years the knowledge that the *Rhapsody* confirmed for an adoring public his place among the masters.

Every discussion of music must, by definition, remain frustratingly outside of the actual experience of listening to music. It is therefore natural for such a discussion to focus, as mine has done in the previous paragraph (and Ross's in his entire book), on all sorts of extra-musical issues. For instance, why do composers write their piece in the first place? How do they feel about their works in that private recess where every creative spirit judges its own creations? What impact does the public success or failure of a piece have on its creator? What then, if not these matters of human interest, should discussion and writing about music be?

In the pursuit of my argument with Alex Ross, what concerns me most about the *Rhapsody* and *Violin Concerto* is their co-coming-into-being — the sense that both works "belong" to the years 1934–35, and not merely to modernism (Berg) or Post-Romanticism (Rachmaninoff), or the rise of Nazism, or the rise of Stalinism. This synchronicity needs to be felt more as a matter of *conviction* than a mere chronological fact, since art works can properly "belong" in spirit to periods very distant from the year of their creation. Still, even the most anachronistic work (either forward- or backward-looking) may be seen as belonging to its own historical moment, reflecting a perverse or wayward aspect of the historical imagination of that moment.

To begin with, following convention, we can agree about the two works that Berg's is the more progressive, and Rachmaninoff's the more conservative. The meanings of these terms have never been entirely clear to me, nor am I sure that there exists a common discourse by which music-loving people employ them. The exact musical *denotations* of the words "progressive" and "conservative" — if such ever existed — have disappeared in our own time into tendentious *connotations*, which are all the more perplexing because their more obvious political applications have so little to do with music. (Here is a signal instance of the disjuncture between music and politics: in the 1930s, Aaron Copland's music became more *conservative* as his politics became more *progressive*.)

When we apply the term "progressive" to the *Violin Concerto*, do we mean that the piece constitutes progress of some sort over previous violin concertos, including Mendelssohn's, Beethoven's, and Brahms's? If so, what sort of progress? A higher level of difficulty for performers? For listeners? What kinds of difficulty? Complexity of harmonic language? A new way of employing the twelve-tone row? Berg's adventurous transformations of classical structures?

Transforming this barrage of questions into statements, we get a fairly accurate description of Berg's achievements in the *Violin Concerto*. But what about beauty? Depth of emotional experience? Need we ask separately about these? What if the technical features of the Concerto are, in fact, directly *responsible* for its beauty and for the ways in which it moves us, without the need for intermediary levels of aesthetic inquiry or mystical meditation . . .?

. . . So they are, resoundingly, they are so! A new kind of beauty and an unprecedented species of emotional profundity appear in the *Violin Concerto*. It is the wedding of traditional technique to innovative spirit which defines the composer's breakthrough. This is the "progress" of the work, which alone makes meaningful the term "progressive."

Now let's turn to the "conservatism" of Rachmaninoff's *Rhapsody on a Theme of Paganini* and to the problems of the word itself. There is a pathological aspect to the term "conservative" in the musical usage of our time. To most composers, it leaves a sour taste in the mouth. Somehow, somewhere along the way — whether in the classroom, the private studio, or the pages of the *New Yorker* — many young composers today have learned to dread the fateful label of "conservative" and equate it with an aesthetic cop-out at worst, temporary insanity at best, and a failure of nerve at all times. Only the epithet of "derivative" more surely casts the fateful *ostrakon*, banishing the offender from the company of authentic composers.

How has this state of affairs come about? Why do so many composers, scholars, and reviewers of concert music today feel such an intense fear — or its obverse, an unseemly pride — of conservatism in their own or the works of others, as well as so much lingering unease for any music in which they detect the odor of it? To be sure, Rachmaninoff is out of favor among college music professors, the only passionate exception known to me being Jay Reise at the University of Pennsylvania.

Let's take a closer look at that dark twin of fear, "unseemly pride." In recent years there has grown a violent reaction by certain composers who have embraced "conservatism" as a self-righteous ideology, dismissing the notion of the avant-garde as obsolete and ironically self-defeating. These meek messiahs who would save themselves and their audiences from the ravages of "squeak-fart music" rashly throw overboard the oars along with the twelve-tone rowboat. Without enlisting the wisdom, energy, and practical lessons from the great music of the twentieth century — regardless of stylistic outlook — these self-styled neo-Romantics find it very hard to return to the safe harbor of tonality or gain rapprochement with audiences. Ideology makes for good argument, not good music. Moreover, general listeners are much more intelligent than many composers give them credit for. Any overture of accessibility on the part of an unknown composer will usually be suspected by the audience (sometimes rightly so) as cynical pandering, or at least as pitiful lack of imagination.

Audiences want to be moved, to have their lives enhanced and enriched. I know this as an avid audience member myself. Most often, concert music fans achieve these rewards through their rendezvous with old familiar friends: Mozart, Verdi, even Stravinsky and Bartók by now, even John Adams. According to one statistic, American orchestras are essentially curators for a "museum" of about 150 pieces, which they recycle over the years. Whom are we to blame for this low number? I, for one, am not going to point the finger. Heaven and Parnassus preserve me from the day I decide I cannot hear the "Prague" Symphony one more time.

So while my generation of composers is busy working out its *meshugas* (untranslatable Yiddish word implying ludicrous thinking or crazy behavior) through various poses on extreme frequencies of the ideological spectrum, sane listeners steer clear of the morass and continue to adore both old and newer masters. But how can composers — who must seek for sanity through their own work — now circumvent the bog of inherited polemic in which they inadvertently find themselves? The principles of psychotherapy dictate that the patient will not conquer fear (or unseemly pride!) unless he or she confronts it. Indulge me, then, as I look the word "conservatism" straight in the "i" (for it is the "-ism" which is always the unhealthiest part of such a word).

I begin with an analogy close to my heart. Reform Judaism began in the nineteenth century as a radical movement in Germany that sought to bring the traditions of the Jewish faith up to date. Inspired by the philosophical investigations of Felix Mendelssohn's grandfather, Moses Mendelssohn — the leader of the Jewish Enlightenment (*Haskalah*) — the founders of the German Reform Temple sought to make Jewish practice ring true to a new, modern age that was vastly different from the period in which the mores and rituals of rabbinical Judaism were established.

The Reform movement swept through the United States in the early part of the twentieth century, but a number of sympathetic American Jews were not altogether happy with the changes. In their perception, beloved values and traditions were threatened by the Reformists' banner cry of "religion for our time." As a result, the Conservative movement of American Judaism was founded — "re-reformed," as it were. In the twenty-first century, the Conservative synagogue continues its efforts to wed the old with the new. No "starting from scratch" is possible here; Conservative Jews (like me) hope to retain what is most cherished from the richness of all the centuries (especially the study of holy texts in their original Hebrew and Aramaic), but we also recognize the need to reconcile tradition with modernity. It is a poignant struggle, sometimes scorned by Orthodox Jews as hypocritical and by Reform Jews as retrogressive. But Conservative Judaism endures, on a precarious ridge thrown up by beleaguering forces all around. Imagine how challenging it is for a Conservative Jew to keep balance in Nashville, the buckle of the Christian Bible Belt. Most of the roofs we would fiddle on (in a bluegrass vein, naturally) are already occupied by steeples. But we scratch away, never from scratch, balancing the beauties of an unattainable past with the uncertainties of a pressing present.

Both Reform Judaism in the United States and the American musical avant-garde are concerned to bring their work into closer accord with the changing world around them, and even to help shape that world. But whereas the Reform temple hopes to help American Jews live *more* comfortably with Judaism, "Reform composers" — among them the preeminent Jews Stefan Wolpe, Milton Babbitt, Ralph Shapey, Leon Kirchner, Morton Feldman, and even Arnold Schoenberg himself in his California years — have always striven to make listeners live *less* comfortably with music.

The founding principles of the American Jewish Conservative movement (they are a far cry from any proselytizing theology, I assure you!) help us to thread a path between these two conflicting modes of amelioration — the overly accommodating and the overly austere — and recognize a happy, unequivocal middle ground. If "conservative" means possessing the desire to *retain what is most cherished from the richness of all the centuries, while recognizing the need to reconcile tradition with modernity*, then the word perfectly suits the Rachmaninoff of the *Rhapsody*.

But wait! Does not the word also give a perfectly good account of the Berg of the *Violin Concerto*?!

Berg's extensive incorporation of a Bach chorale into the Concerto would be too glib a way to prove the "conservatism" of the work. Besides, quotation technique in itself is not a guarantee of a conservative ethic. Through quotation, the third movement of Luciano Berio's *Sinfonia* (1969) goes a long way towards demonstrating that what follows upon direct confrontation with masterworks of earlier eras is not conservative balance or a sane regard for the past, but rather disorientation, spiritual fragmentation and madness. As I remarked in my Preface, it is the *spirit* in which composers do things that matters most in assessing their achievements.

In keeping with his ethereal dedication to "the memory of an angel" (Berg's young friend Manon Gropius, the daughter of Alma Mahler, who died in April of 1935 at the age of 18), Berg constructs his tone row so that the final four notes of the series correspond to the first four notes of a haunting Lutheran chorale melody set by Bach. Towards the end of the *Concerto*, the centuries-old chorale comes into focus, but never sharply: a halo of dissonant counterpoint surrounds it, lending it an almost painterly blur. The modern gently attends upon the ancient, in the character of an Adoration. With reverent acquiescence, Berg holds out a groping hand from his own existential position and a higher power serenely takes hold of it.

It is an *affront*, this surrender by Berg to Bach, on the common ground of technique and spirit, just as any breakthrough of genius against orthodoxy is an affront. With sublime irony, the "orthodoxy" violated here is modernism itself. A breach of the concerto's twelve-tone propriety, the arrival of Bach radically alters the sound of the concerto in midstream. It is a moment of searing *conservative* insight, which gives ineffable meaning to all the "progressive" music of the *Concerto* that has come before. Going even further, one could say that the quotation itself constitutes "progress" of a highest sort; for there is an unprecedented shock in the profoundly seamless transition of Berg into Bach and Bach back into Berg. Never before or since have two such different composers met face to face on such equal terms. Alex Ross could have more effectively launched his book with this enduring encounter in music, rather than the brief meeting in the flesh between Berg and Gershwin.

Now I will try to turn the tables: if Berg's *Violin Concerto* is a "conservative" work in the best sense of the term, then could not Rachmaninoff's popular Rhapsody be "progressive" in some way? If a thoughtful, though still vague, definition of "progress" could be "a new kind of beauty or a new kind of emotional experience," can we not see the *Rhapsody on a Theme of Paganini* in this light? By no means is the form of the work new. The virtuosic theme and variations for soloist and orchestra had already served many composers well, from Mozart to Tchaikovsky. What of Rachmaninoff's variation technique? The theme is presented in a manner vividly reminiscent of the finale of Beethoven's "Eroica" Symphony: after a brief but portentous introduction we do not at first hear Paganini's famous theme, but rather a series of isolated notes that leap by octave and fifth. In the Classical coin of musical economy, Rachmaninoff beats Beethoven at his own melodic game. The sparse opening statement is not a "point" to the Paganini tune's "counterpoint," but rather an actual *skeleton* of the tune itself. The bounding notes deliver a cross section of the tune, sounding intermittently on an implied graph of its not-yet-audible melodic contour. Paganini remains embryonic so that Rachmaninoff can spring forth fully armed from the *Rhapsody*'s first leaping notes.

Rachmaninoff's choice of the Paganini caprice melody boldly and calculatedly invites comparison with the torrent of variation sets on the very same tune by composers past and future (Brahms and Lutoslawski, most notably). The piece therefore expands into a yet more complex kind of historical conversation, in what might be called "variations on variations." This involvement with the history of music — not just his immediate Romantic inheritance, but the whole stretch of usable past (as in his splendid *Corelli Variations*, or his preoccupation with the Gregorian *Dies irae* chant) — typifies Rachmaninoff's compositional attitude. The adjective "contrapuntal" characterizes very well both his historical imagination and his idiosyncratic musical textures, which are the most dedicated revisions of old-fashioned counterpoint since Brahms. Rachmaninoff is backward-looking; but his "looking backward" is done for the sake of a fierce stylistic consistency, whereby the composer is at once faithful to his sources of inspiration and to his own peculiar self (yet another resemblance to Brahms). Whatever one may think of Rachmaninoff's harmonic and melodic idiom — and Alex Ross literally thinks nothing of it in his book, poor fellow — it is as immediately recognizable as any of the Classic or Romantic masters. Ironically, the same cannot be said of Berg's style, which has suffered the inevitable collapse of radical artistic breakthrough into academic convention. So "progressive" was Berg's harmonic language that it has voraciously been devoured by generations of composers around the world, down to our own day. How many countless times have I had occasion to say of a new piece of academic music that "it sounds like Berg"? The progenitor has been overwhelmed by its own spawn. Twenty-first-century American university professors and their students composing post-World War I Viennese angst . . . go figure.

Rachmaninoff's style, however, was so immediately recognizable and its effects so measurable to its first audiences, that it suffered from an entirely different problem. Ever since Hollywood composers got hold of the Rachmaninoff sound in the 1930s and '40s, audience members in the symphony concert hall have responded to Rachmaninoff's music itself with a bizarre reversal of causality: "This Rachmaninoff piece sounds like movie music." So pervasive was Rachmaninoff's influence on American culture that the ever-present "pomposers" who deemed commercial entertainment the enemy of authentic art disliked his music as a matter of course, branding him as an accomplice in the general cultural decline.

In short, Rachmaninoff became a household name in the middle decades of the twentieth century. My late friend Sterling Lanier remembers seeing the Russian giant perform right here in Nashville, on the very same stage which made Hank Williams famous. This phenomenal success is something that a certain class of "serious" music lovers can never forgive him for. Just as they feel there must be something wrong with a public that now makes a multimillionaire out of the 15-year-old Justin Bieber, so do they feel that there must be something wrong with Rachmaninoff, who was made a millionaire by an earlier version of the same mindless public while Alban Berg was struggling to make ends meet.

I will never understand composers who pretend not to need or desire — or who actually disdain — public acceptance (on his part, Berg dearly hoped for it). It is a terrible kind of self-loathing that allows only the self to adore itself, perhaps along with a few chosen acolytes. The elitist self-consciousness and insecurity of composers — the desperately smug awareness of their own intellectual and spiritual superiority — has been one of the most pernicious forces in our academic musical culture. One of my recent graduates believed himself to be so talented (and he was, bless his heart) that he did not want to sully his music's purity with an audience. He was playing his own cold little glass-bead game. I implored him carefully to consider Mozart, who was exemplary in self-awareness and resourcefulness. Mozart saw himself not as *better* than, but as *equal* to his audience (of whichever class). His music neither condescended to nor alienated his patrons, no matter what their social status. And contrary to persistent myth, Mozart was on the whole delighted by its reception through most of his career. My clever student pointed out to me that Mozart's naïve trust in his public probably drove him to his death. I told him that there were worse ways to die — namely forgotten, and besides one shot of antibiotics would have saved the good fellow. Will composers today ever learn from Mozart to see themselves as *equals* to a public who hungers for music it can love?

Close study of the structural and gestural nature of Rachmaninoff's *Rhapsody* reinforces the conclusion that "progress" is not what this piece is about. It does not give us a new kind of beauty, nor is it really a different kind of emotional experience from the kind we enjoy in, say, Tchaikovsky's music. Detractors will claim (if they even bother to say anything at all, which Ross does not) that this familiarity of Romantic gesture is the primary reason for the work's enduring popularity. Even the most ingenious and justly famous passage — in which Rachmaninoff inverts Paganini's melody with Baroque strictness and Schumannesque abandon — clearly draws much of its dazzle and power from the finale of Tchaikovsky's Piano Concerto No. 1.

Rachmaninoff does indeed employ the standard Post-Romantic device of *sweeping-tune-with-grandiose-climax-as-apotheosis-with-struggle* (there's probably a single German word for that). But, much like Elgar's "Nimrod" variation in his *Enigma Variations*, the big tune is not the big finish. Both Elgar and Rachmaninoff set themselves a difficult Romantic problem, long familiar to us from Berlioz's fantastic guillotine straight through Strauss's Zarathustran rebirth: how can you get things going again after such a rip-roaring climax?

You don't have to read a sex manual to answer the question. All you have to do is listen to Elgar and Rachmaninoff (I have never been sure that Strauss pulls it off in *Also Sprach Zarathustra*). Immediately following the magnificent "Nimrod," Elgar provides the proverbial cigarette in bed, a sly and insouciant variation on his theme. In the *Rhapsody* (here, the title's implication of eccentricity becomes most eloquent), Rachmaninoff takes a page or two right out of Berlioz's *Symphonie fantastique*: his "big finish" (the big tune) gives way to a *danse macabre*, through whose wild bounding the medieval *Dies Irae* chant confesses to having been composed in some prior incarnation by Berlioz's Mephistophelean pal Paganini.

Gregorian chant & Berlioz & Paganini masquerading as Rachmaninoff & Co.; Carinthian folk song & Bach chorale doing service as Berg & Co.: Ezra Pound's poetics of *personae* consistently functions as twentieth-century artists' compulsive way to be original, no matter what their stylistic preoccupations.

But Schumann was already defining himself out of his company of embodied *personae* in the Second Symphony. Would it then be fair to say that the spirit of the twentieth century dawned in Schumann's Second? It would be better to get rid of the zeitgeist altogether (lay the ghost!) and instead just pay attention to the ties that bind composers together, whoever and whenever they are.

Synchronous relationships are exceedingly complicated; I can understand why Alex Ross ignores them. Berg and Rachmaninoff do not "hold hands" across their obvious aesthetic divide merely because they are both working in the years 1934–35. Rachmaninoff is obviously closer in sound to Schumann than to Berg. But all three composers deploy *personae* at crucial structural moments, audible signs of the debt they are paying to the spiritual reservoirs of past music. It is academically useful to distinguish Berg as someone who uses "modernist" means to this end, and Rachmaninoff as someone who uses "post-Romantic" ones. Ross takes little occasion to observe either obvious divergences or subtler connections of this sort. I was inclined to say that this is a pity; but, more accurately, the omission of a synchronous sensibility shows his *lack of pity* for those many readers who will always have greater need for Rachmaninoff than for Berg.

The *Rhapsody* builds towards its ending in a manner every lover of Romantic music hopes for and cherishes. There is a crashing penultimate flourish on the *Dies Irae*, followed by a predictable shift to a brighter harmony. Everything is ready for a booming final cadence, Rachmaninoff's signature in warhorse after warhorse . . .

. . . but it never happens. Instead, silence, then pianist alone, pianissimo, with a fragment of the first phrase of the Paganini theme — the part that happens to be a perfect cadence — and the piece is over. In the context of Rachmaninoff's style and of the building momentum of the *Rhapsody's* final section, nothing could be more unexpected than this understated quietus. The economy of using the motive of the caprice, the stunning simplicity of the harmony, the symmetrical delight we take in the theme's first notes turning into the work's last notes, the hush of the lone piano drawing the piece to a close — all these factors combine to summon up a cathartic burst of feeling: we are forced, on whatever level of awareness, instantaneously to "explain" to ourselves the discrepant event of this surprise soft ending. A whirlwind of information must be processed in order to account for this ultimate, conclusive departure from stylistic convention. Oh, how the thinking mind empowers the feeling heart in the last few seconds of Rachmaninoff's *Rhapsody*! It is this wedding of heart and mind (celebrated again later in Chapter 6) which justifies my teacher Jay Reise's claim that Rachmaninoff is the one of the few genuine heirs of J. S. Bach in the twentieth century — an outrageous claim for almost every other academic composer, especially to those who point more obviously and unimaginatively to the literal quotation of Bach in Berg's *Violin Concerto*.

At the core of all music we call "serious" is the element of *playfulness*. The sudden wake-up call in Haydn's *Surprise Symphony* is only the most blatant example of how composers manipulate our expectations and shock us out of our complacency, as all good comedy does. In the works of the Baroque, Classic, Romantic, and Modernist eras (grouped together as "classical," by iTunes consensus), *the character of a musical idea is never fixed*. Understand this essential feature of classical music and you are well on your way to understanding how it differs from popular music. In pop music, expressive power inheres in a musical figure's redundancy and fixity of character. But in classical music, we generally cannot predict how the same theme will turn up next. Just as our friends continually surprise us with new versions of themselves, so too the working-out of a theme in classical music is the ongoing revelation of what that theme *is* through *what it can do*. In life, as in art, the qualities of wit and economy are what make such ingenious adaptability possible. New rules are devised for the game at the turning of every corner. Like Indiana Jones, composers do not break rules; they make 'em up as they go along. Spontaneous risks thus become blueprints of inevitability.

Rachmaninoff take grapes from the old vines of Romanticism — irrevocably going fallow in his time — and squeezes them into his new and well-fermented wine. Berg is less sanguine about his appropriations; in order to pass into the *terra incognita* he stakes out for himself, he carries Bach with him as a talisman, not as a viable map. The enormous differences between the *Rhapsody* and the *Violin Concerto* in attitude, resources and sheer sound, drive us headlong once again into the question: how can *both* works be "representative" of the 12-month period in 1934–35 in which they appeared?

It has been tempting for music history textbooks to answer the question with some version of anthropological succession: Rachmaninoff is Neanderthal man, pathetically surviving beyond his own epoch, coexisting with a more advanced species, watching his way of life die all around him, while Berg is the burgeoning *Homo sapiens*, bolder, smarter, more technologically capable, his innocence gone.

I have sworn off this sort of stylistic Darwinism, which motivates the "starting-from-scratch" narrative of modernism I laid out in the earlier section and serves as its founding law — the closest thing we will ever get to a zeitgeist. I recited this *tabula rasa* tale not because I harbor any illusion of its objective historical validity, but because *it describes the abiding habit of mind of the modernist composers themselves.* A masterpiece of subjectivity and tendentiousness, the modernist narrative only goes so far in accounting for the synchronous whirlwind of twentieth-century music. Our two composers Alban and Sergei are of the same generation. Both were born and raised in the nineteenth century. Both accepted that century's musical legacy fully, while willfully misinterpreting it — as every mature person must misinterpret a childhood legacy whose conditions have gone extinct. Berg seized upon twelve-tone music and cinematic dramaturgy as congenial ways in which to update the transformative promises of Romanticism and face the brutal exigencies of his own time. Rachmaninoff perceived that in order to face those same brutalities — which he, as a Russian exile, suffered as much as anyone — he and his audiences needed to *keep* the healing and transformative promises of Romanticism — promises made by Chopin, Liszt, and Tchaikovsky, all of whom would have recognized Rachmaninoff as their belated brother, and pitied him for believing so devotedly in their broken word, their broken song.

Composers, music journalists and all other flawed human beings stand to learn much from considering Berg's *Concerto* and Rachmaninoff's *Rhapsody* in the fortuitous light of each other. *Make it well,* enjoin both works. *Make it beautiful; make it from what you know best, but do not count on that "what" to mean the same thing in your hands. Take risks; they are worth it. There may or may not be so-called progress in what you do, but make it so that you can be proud of it, so that players will want to play it and hearers hear it. What you make may look mostly backwards or mostly forwards, it does not matter which; or it may be a magnificent Janus that can open doors and silence doomsayers and greet the world with reasonable fearfulness and irrational hope.*

Think about the years 1934–35 for a moment: think, as Alex Ross so magisterially does, of their horrific waves of Nazism and Stalinism (our composers' compatriots responsible for these); the lingering Depression; a continent still under the shadow of one world war, stunned into helplessness as that very same shadow darkened towards another. How dare we speak of progress in art when humanity was reverting to inconceivable barbarity? Can aesthetic discourse be so far removed from historical reality and still be meaningful? Touched deeply by events around them, confused as anybody about what the future held, Berg and Rachmaninoff managed to do in these two glorious works what it is the right and responsibility of every unpolluted soul to do which has recognized its own creative gift: to give it back, unstintingly, so it will help anoint in joyful sorrow other souls whom the world has touched too deeply and to whom the future is terribly uncertain.

Third question: How to redress Alex Ross's wrongful neglect of (at least) Ralph Vaughan Williams, without merely expressing a subjective grievance about what his book excludes? I take Ross at his Preface's disclaiming word (he makes it clear that The Rest Is Noise *does not pretend to give a comprehensive account), so I will not settle for anything less than a principle of historical consciousness. How to hold up the music of Vaughan Williams (and of his spiritual ally Béla Bartók) as an audible sign of a more desirable largesse than Ross's for "listening to the twentieth century"?*

III. THE ANGLO FILES

As I write this, I am somewhere over Arizona, on my way to San Francisco to lecture on "Hey Jude" and Beethoven's Ninth at the Moscone Center. The pilot just announced that we are directly above Monument Valley. It is a perfectly clear day, so I can see every dot of sagebrush congregating around every arroyo. We have no music worthy of this landscape. John Denver sang sweetly of the nearby peaks; but in "Rocky Mountain High," he feels good about his beloved hills without acknowledging their awesome power. Ferde Grofé's *Grand Canyon Suite* makes for delightful musical tourism, donkey ride and all; but the diversions of "burro-ing" down into the canyon have little to do with the pleasures of casting the imagination down into the canyon's deep geological time. It is largely because this terrain is so inhospitable to human life that it could never have engendered a repertoire of indigenous song, apart from the great Native-American rituals that have sprung up here over long centuries.

The austerity of the American wilderness — whether the Rockies or the Smokies — has kept our folk music relatively simple, straightforward, no-nonsense, no occasion for the rhythmic adventures of Latin music, no room to sing and dance but on a front porch or in a cleared-out barn. Before Aaron Copland could find a way to make Billy the Kid's prairie or Martha Graham's homestead come to musical life, he first had to travel south of the border, where he found that every arid Mexican village and smoky salon had its own rich store of syncopated song. It is no accident, then, that our comparatively bland folk music has always lent itself to a peculiarly urban twist, when a sophisticated city Jew like Copland or Richard Rodgers imagines what it might feel like to sleep out under the stars or ride a horse past a cornfield in Oklahoma.

The countryside of the British Isles tells a different, impressively tuneful story. It is almost impossible to investigate a single hill or valley in England, Wales or Scotland without coming across some folk song or singsong verse associated with that elevation or declivity. For many years, my wife and I spent a week or two every summer (and once an entire semester) on Dartmoor in southwest England — not in the famous prison, but on the moor itself, so much more beautiful and sun-drenched than Arthur Conan Doyle pretends it to be in *The Hound of the Baskervilles*. Although we were really just long-term tourists, once in a rare while I would meet up with an old moorman, a scapegrace son of a Dartmoor household, who, when he learned I was a musician, reeled off a strain or two of Devonshire song from his childhood for me in his cracked voice.

Alex Ross has little interest in this ethnographic heart of so much twentieth-century music, what is grandiloquently called "ethnomusicology" by the academy, the primal source of Igor Stravinsky's genius, Béla Bartók's, Ralph Vaughan Williams', and to a lesser degree — because on less cultivated soil — Aaron Copland's. Even in the chapter he devotes to Sibelius, it is not so much the ethnographic wizardry of the composer that concerns Ross (he even takes an occasion here to belittle this element as "folk realism") as Sibelius' *renunciation* of wizardry, his Prospero-like breaking of his magic staff, his forgotten, now-unimaginable popularity.

If you listen closely to the twentieth century, you will hear — as yet one more binding narrative that Ross ignores — over and over again the death knell of nearly every musical folkway in Europe, from Siberia to the Outer Hebrides. What did the doomed cultural capital of European folk traditions — devastated by industrialization and war — mean to the great composers who drew upon them? Various things, depending on the spirit of the composer. From a technical point of view, both Bartók and Vaughan Williams understood that a very dramatic way to effect a musical *tabula rasa* for the new century was to wash the slate raw in a cauldron of non-Western musical lye — asymmetrical meters, exotic modes and all — perhaps boiled up by one of the countless old crones they met on their walking tours of the villages of Transylvania or East Anglia.

But both of them also hoped for something more than that: through their "concerted efforts" of symphonic and chamber music, the Magyar and the Englishman both strove to give the peasantry an authentic voice — always with due pessimism, always with the sober conviction that at the very least, the political powerlessness of the husbandman was matched by that of the composer. There was no possible way for Bartók or Vaughan Williams to embody in the concert hall the actual voices of peasants — those voices they took down in dictation on their walking tours. But they were both driven by an ethical impulse to be true to those strange voices by virtue of the essential strangeness of their own musical craft.

The *ethics* of folk-inflected music in the twentieth century transcends the Romantic nationalism of nineteenth-century composers like Dvorak and Rimsky-Korsakov (and their belated heir Sibelius). In the twentieth century, nothing less was at stake for Vaughan Williams and Bartók than the preservation — at least in music — of a soon-to-be-extinct culture. Both men refused honors that their countries tried to heap upon them — honorary doctorates, knighthood — insisting that their regard for folk music had nothing to do with national interest and everything to do with the rights of human beings, no matter who, to live freely and fully the cultural identities bestowed on them by their parents and their communities, whether Hungarian, Bulgarian, Devonian or Ordovician (how lovely to be able to use these latter two geological names for their pristine geographical designations of regions in England and Wales).

Alex Ross crudely dismisses Ralph Vaughan Williams and Bartók as "folkish," when to be "folkish" is to be the tragically hopeful delegate for the population of nine-tenths of the land-mass of Europe. It is the curse of every critical mind to treat with contempt the *pastoral* as mere *pastime*. In Vaughan Williams' short piece for violin and orchestra, *The Lark Ascending*, the lark ascends, and the Empson- or Adorno-ridden philosopher says, "Phooey!" I plead guilty myself, not least because my English friend Peter reminds me of an ornithological fact that Vaughan Williams fails to appreciate in his flight of lyrical fancy: what the lark is really saying while ascending, with mindless redundancy, is "GO AWAY, GO AWAY FROM MY NEST, GO AWAY, GO AWAY *RIGHT NOW*." Not very lyrical, that.

Every university music teacher of mine who condescended to say anything at all about Vaughan Williams in class did so with unveiled distaste, or even chagrin, blaming him (and/or Rachmaninoff) for the glut of plagiarizing John Williamses in Hollywood. Just as Sibelius suffered an academic backlash from enjoying loads of air time in the 1930s and '40s (as Ross points out), Vaughan Williams was the enemy of music professors in the 1970s and '80s because he was the darling of classical DJs (another almost-extinct species).

My mentors were pissed off at Vaughan Williams for being too listenable on the radio. If one lives long enough, it is possible (but not guaranteed) that one may rise above such pettiness, both from others and in oneself. My mentors were wise on every other matter (as you shall see in the next chapter), but they were blind to the possibility that an accessible composer could be a good composer *on the ground of his accessibility*, rather than on the arcane ground of a complexity hidden beneath an accessible surface (as in Handel, Mozart, Chopin, etc.).

Few detractors of Vaughan Williams who have shoved aside *The Lark Ascending* have ever thought to study closely his Fourth Symphony instead, a cry ascending far higher than the lark's call, composed against the precipitous ascent of fascism in the 1930s. It is not just unfair, it is ridiculous to reject *The Lark Ascending* without considering the intelligence with which Vaughan Williams reveals in his Fourth what happens to blithely singing nature and pastorally wondering humanity during a bleak crisis. The strung-out second theme of the first movement is a folk song gone *nutters*, an ascending lark maniacally transmuted into a swooping buzzard. Why didn't Vaughan Williams accept a knighthood from King George? Because *this* is what kings and prime ministers perpetrate, this unholy corruption of the land and its inhabitants into targets for warplanes — doomed, unsingable, and silenced forever.

The infernal metamorphosis of Vaughan Williams' typical folk manner, dramatically played out in the Fourth Symphony, is one of the musical wonders of the twentieth century. Things get even more tenebrous in the Sixth, one of the most dissonant pieces of symphonic music ever written — in the original sense of dissonance's taking energy from a fragile, untenable, *audible* consonance. Standing between these two shaky pillars of the Fourth and the Sixth is the greensward of the Fifth Symphony, sown by Vaughan Williams during the darkest hours of World War II: a *proper* pastoral, the poetic mode that always veers more or less vertiginously towards grief (*Et in Arcadia Ego*). In the closing pages of the Fifth Symphony, a common stream of dance music (an old-fashioned ground bass) flows out into broad meadows of pure D major, not a single added sharp or flat in sight for miles. Throughout the orchestra, the English downs seem to swell in their mild and chalky splendor, all of it perfectly enduring, all of it perfectly lost to our post-pastoral minds. There is a difference between nostalgia and lament. While *nostalgia* misses the beloved place and pathetically makes it sad, *lament* grieves over the beloved place and necessarily makes it glad — just what happens at traditional English wakes (as well as Finnegans).

We can only hope for anything, if we can grieve for it. This is as true for the planet we live on as it is for the love we bear towards someone we have lost. A pedagogy of grief enables a grammar of hope — a very different kind of "starting from scratch" than the modernists had in mind. *Optimism is just as much an enemy of hope as pessimism.* If you expect (or are forced to expect) things to get better of their own accord, then there is little reason for you to work actively and hopefully towards that amelioration. Two great symphonic contemporaries of Vaughan Williams provide a useful contrast to his hopefulness. Sibelius was optimistic in an old-fashioned manner, according to the set dictates of the Finnish legends: nature *will* endure, in spite of foolish humanity. Shostakovich was an optimist by force, in the ultra-modern manner, through political and mortal necessity. Both composers constructed workable myths for their oppressed compatriots, one out of a nature-saturated mysticism and the other out of an ingenious manipulation of Communist ideology — and both always under the Russian gun.

Meanwhile, Ralph Vaughan Williams would not touch a myth with a ten-foot maypole. He and Bartók both intuited that myths become infinitely corruptible when unmoored from a viable folk tradition (the word *unmoored* has a special ring for me and my own fragile Devon landscape). Myths are incapable of raising the cry that always ascends from Vaughan Williams' song: *Dona nobis pacem.* He and Bartók knew, in their divergent ways, that there would never be an answer to this prayer from on high — only the one they could give listeners through their beautiful music, the source of my gladness in giving you this little bit of the rest of *The Rest Is Noise.*

Fourth question: How to unfold at least one garment from Ross's breezy laundry list of late twentieth-century composers, so that we can hold it up to the light, see how it has weathered the winds of changing musical fashion, and try it on for size? How to encourage a habit of mind whereby a listener takes the time and the trouble to enjoy the "invisible men and women" of the late twentieth century, those brilliant concert composers who have become all the more difficult to discover as our new century pursues its unbearable lightness of musical being? How to reveal at least one palette of distinctive colors in the latter quarter of the century, when all sorts of thrilling extensions and renunciations of modernism — as Ross himself has demonstrated admirably in various New Yorker reviews — helped to define the 1900s as surely as anything earlier, by the author's beloved "conspiracy of S's" Schoenberg, Shostakovich or Strauss (Strauss, for pity's sake!)? Of all people, the new-music champion Ross could have realized that when a magazine journalist makes his star turn — writing a full-length book for a wider-reaching readership — he has a special opportunity, if not obligation, to provide information and insight readers may not be able to find anywhere else about exciting music that is less accessible in every way (recentness, recording availability, etc.). And I will extend my Anglophilia one step further: why would a critic who has lavished thousands of words of praise on the living British composer Thomas Adès in the pages of the New Yorker turn his back on Adès in The Rest Is Noise, devoting a meager hundred words or so on the composer's fine music? Hamlet's original dying words seem more fitting for the title of Ross's book: The rest is silence. Could such exclusions have been a matter of editorial constraints? Surely, we could have done with three or four fewer anecdotes about Richard Strauss (whom, make no mistake, I love to transfiguring death), in favor of more than just one bare sentence about Adès's stupendous symphonic work Asyla. Let alone Ross's absolute silence over works by the elder Brits Tippett, Birtwistle, Maxwell Davies, Matthews, Ferneyhough — blimey, there are loads more, too. Ross's book gives no clue (perhaps he has no clue) about the thriving, complex, current state of concert music in the UK (ironically at odds with Adès's own superstar status), a

product of the intelligence and commitment of visionary perform-
ers and programmers. The grievance intensifies on our own side of
the pond, in a country where the idea of a national radio station
devoted to classical music (like Britain's BBC 3) is as fantastical as
— well, as the notion of a black president passing national health-
care reform legislation. In other words, there is always hope. And
so, dear reader, I pluck for you, out of Ross's cold, cold laundry list,
one of my favorite pieces to clothe my hopeful spirit in, inviting you
to keep warm and dry in it, too.

IV. ULYSSES IN CAMBRIDGE, MASSACHUSETTS

Pulitzer Prize, MacArthur Foundation "genius" award, American
Academy of Arts and Letters fellowship, professorship at MIT,
unending commissions and all, composer John Harbison is a
genuine "insider" — perhaps *the* insider — in the American
concert music biz. But somehow, with the same mysterious
grace to be found in his finest music, John does not seem to be
touched by all that racket. He is one of the most serene, most
interior persons I have ever met, all the more so because of his
great and obvious passions. Of the dozens of composers I've
met who keep open the "shop" of contemporary classical music,
Harbison is one of only two who never talk shop, who refuse
to talk shop (the other one is George Crumb). All John wants
to do is talk about great music (like Schumann's Second on my
car radio). With uncanny exactitude, Harbison's best works do
the same thing: they "talk" about great music; more than that,
they argue directly with the masters, in the same party spirit as
Schumann's gutsy finale. Sometimes friendly, sometimes vexed,
sometimes supplicating, Harbison's musical "conversations" with
Bach, Schubert, and Stravinsky (three of his favorites) work the
same miracle Schumann did in his Second Symphony, a miracle properly expressed in Bach-tinged Latin: *quarens altros,*

inveniet ipsum; seeking out others, Harbison finds himself.

At certain moments of structural crisis in John's music — they happen in every piece — you can feel his whole musical being drop spread-eagled onto the ground, pressing his ear against it, listening, *listening* for the still-untapped musical springs flowing beneath, which are ready to bubble up at the right touch from the right composer's divining rod. Harbison has the carriage and dignity of knowing he is a colleague of Bach, a friend to Schubert, an interlocutor with Stravinsky, their ally as well as their disciple. No surprise, then, that John is well known in the Boston area as a conductor of Bach's sacred works.

Harbison wanders, at home in the sea of classical music. He is both the careening dolphin of the Greek myth *and* the Amphion singing for his passage on the dolphin's back; for there is always in John's music the need for one character to expand into two, for melody to become counterpoint, for consonance and dissonance to fashion a new dialectic. *At home, at sea*: this is Harbison's imaginative template. As he reflected some years ago in a published article, the composer of contemporary concert music naturally possesses something of the character of Coleridge's Ancient Mariner, the haunted creature who detains the guest from the wedding feast with his harrowing tale — just as the living composer harrows the concertgoer, detaining him from the Tchaikovsky on the second half of the program (as if Tchaikovsky were any less harrowing, if we only paid attention!).

In this marine light, it makes sense that one of John's best works is *Ulysses' Bow* (the second act of his Homeric ballet *Ulysses*, from 1983). No one in the imagination of the Western world works harder to earn his song — or his bed — than Ulysses. Harbison lays open the Ithacan king's desperate labors to reclaim his throne and his long-suffering queen, in a ravishing inventory of orchestral tableaux. The ingenious permutation throughout the ballet of the same handful of themes fulfills the principle of "developing variations," coined by Arnold Schoenberg to describe Johannes Brahms's music. Deliberately at work in scene after scene, then, is a subterranean revision of Romantic consciousness, of a piece with the Tennysonian cadence of the hero's name Ulysses for the ballet, instead of the original Greek form Odysseus. No need to send in Tchaikovsky — he's already here, in music as tuneful in its own way, and as luminously orchestrated, as anything in *Sleeping Beauty*.

In the final scene comes Ulysses' reunion with Penelope, as inevitable and surprising as it is in Homer. The mystery of enduring love rises from the music like archaic incense, a chemistry of sounds shifting restlessly between harmony and discord. With discretion and economy, a spectrum of tonal color ranges across the orchestra. The curtain Homer draws across these two great lovers — who now root themselves in each other as surely as their oak bed roots itself in the earth of Ithaca — can be heard as a curtain of dissonance the music draws over its own thwarted cadence. After all, how *could* the music ever compete with the epic enormity of Ulysses' homecoming? It would have been rank folly, sheer redundancy, for the music to attempt a corresponding tonal resolution.

Harbison makes a proper reckoning of the physical and spiritual cost of this reunion for both Odysseus and Penelope (*you can hear what this music cost him* — this is what John said to me of Schumann in the car). In a master stroke entirely his own, Harbison delivers into our hearing what Wagner could not, what Verdi never once hazarded, what Mozart never stinted to offer up: the mingled joy and sorrow of mortal love — not poisoned, not immured in an Egyptian tomb, not murdered or self-destroying, but simply *mortal*, alive against all the odds, alive against all the gods.

Near the end, the violins sweep from chord to chord, wailing like the piteous ghosts of Ulysses' sailors, audibly present here in the bedroom but unable to touch the exhausted king in his serene and interior joy with Penelope. His hands — just now washed of suitors' blood — now at last take gentle hold of hers. The orchestra swells in cadence after cadence, each one approaching some kind of harmonic closure, but then sheering off from it, as if such resolution were a Scylla or Charybdis to sail right on past. Ulysses' bow bends towards Eros', the sensual shimmer of the music rounded and voluptuous.

And now comes the exquisite final touch: a soft, sustained sorting of unsettled harmonies, a sonority beloved of Harbison and often present in the music of his heroes (e.g., Bach's Brandenburg Concerto No. 1 and Stravinsky's *Symphony of Psalms*). This stark, almost too-simple chorale looks forward to Harbison's masterpiece, *The Most Often Used Chords* (1993), an orchestral work slyly based on the "found object" of a manual for composers discovered by John on the inside cover of an Italian music manuscript notebook.

Harbison gives a *summa poetica* of the whole ballet in these closing chords. So few artists of this or any era have the skill and depth of spirit to achieve a perfect balance of *techné* and *pathos*. Homer sets the bar very high in the first place. For once in the late twentieth century, a composer leaps right over it. Don't listen to Alex Ross on the late twentieth century. Listen to John Harbison.

Chapter 5

Daimones

Your song, what does it know?

Paul Celan

As luck would have it, I worked closely in college with three of the most significant late twentieth-century composers of concert music. George Crumb and Richard Wernick had both earned the Pulitzer Prize for music, and it was something of a scandal that George Rochberg had not also received it. In my first three years at the University of Pennsylvania, I was a pre-med student taking music courses for the fun of it. Little by little, my teachers showed me just how serious this fun could be. My career in medicine dissolved in a concentrated solution of Bach, Beethoven, Brahms, Bartók, and a bushel of other composers whose names did or did not begin with the letter B.

I knew almost nothing about my three mentors or their music while I was studying with them. Now, 30 years on, I own and cherish dozens of their recordings and I regularly include their music in the courses I teach. I have hosted two of them at my music school. Rochberg died in 2005, but we were in close touch right up to the end. It's good to know I can drop a line to Crumb or Wernick any time, just to say hello, just to say "thank you." But I don't do this often enough (now you know the main reason for this chapter).

In their personal lives, Crumb, Wernick, and Rochberg have almost nothing in common with each other. It is well-known that two of them were not even on speaking terms with the third for years. But they share a singular quality — something I am afraid to trivialize with a concrete name. It is not an attitude; nor is it a belief. Call it, rather, a *hunch*. It goes something like this. Not a poem. Just a little stream of wondering:

> *The great music of any time or place*
> *has a deathless spirit.*
> *Such music is as fresh today*
> *as it was*
> *when the notes were still wet*
> *on the page or on the lips.*
> *Its language is*
> *above all*
> *intuitive,*
> *irrational,*
> *in touch with*
> *the least accessible sources*
> *of human feeling.*
> *Differences in historical style*
> *bear witness to the spirit,*
> *showing how supple it is*
> *and how variously it can be*
> *embodied.*
> *A Bach prelude*
> *and a Debussy prelude*
> *are separated*
> *by almost two centuries,*
> *but they are closer to each other*

than we are
to yesterday's newspaper.
The dates on the composer's tombstone
do not matter,
for deathless music
always inhabits the present . . .
No, no! It's more than that!
Enduring art of any sort
is nothing less than *the present —*
the one reality that never can be past or future.
Whenever we love,
whenever we suffer
or enjoy —
and when, in the end, we die —
the spirit precedes us,
leads us,
buoys us,
enfolds us.
Some people call the spirit
God.
Music
needs no name for it.

Back when I was their student, George, Dick, and George
understood very well that their hunch belonged to a current of
artistic insight that was steadily drying up, while also running
against a tide of cultural relativism and contingency. Aside
from being old-fashioned, politically incorrect and historically
improbable, their idea was also terribly difficult to pitch to 18- or
20-year-olds (like me), who in the surreal, Reagan-clouded 1980s
were mainly concerned with consuming the latest album by The
Talking Heads, Madonna, or Michael Jackson.

None of my three teachers actually came out and *spoke* the
hunch straightforwardly. Rather, they wore it like a mantle; it
colored all their speech; it infiltrated their classrooms like light.

It was written on their faces, in the way they carried themselves, in their rare but precious laughter.

It pleases me to imagine that in the context of early Christianity, these three men — two of them Jewish — would have been saints. I'm not just putting my teachers up on a pedestal. If anything, I am trying to bring them down to earth, to *understand* them through the analogy, which suggests that they, like the saints of old, could not help but believe in their hunch, that it defined them, uplifted them, and that they suffered on account of it.

They suffered on account of it. In my classes and private lessons with them, I discovered that the principles linking Rochberg, Wernick, and Crumb to each other, and binding them together into something that could rightly be called a "school," came back again and again to one vexing notion: music as a spiritual ordeal of some kind — a *passion*, in the religious sense. Whatever piece we were looking at together, sooner or later the discussion turned to questions I would sooner have skipped:

> At what spiritual cost did this music come into being?
> How did it pay for its hold upon truth?

These are the hard, intractable questions John Harbison, a fourth great mentor, was holding in his mind and holding out to me, when we were listening to Schumann's Second together on the car radio. They are really the same question that Paul Celan poses in one of the final poems he wrote before throwing himself to death in the Seine: *Your song, what does it know?*

As I look back on the fortunate time I spent with my triumvirate, I realize that this question was the ground of all our conversations. I could not readily hear the question in my college days, let alone attempt to answer it. I knew so little about anything, except for my own youthful hungers — and surely nothing about spiritual ordeals. All I could do, then, was to take down an inkling in my callow shorthand and store it up, so that I could redeem it when it — and I — matured.

His task is . . .
To register cataclysm in a single pitch;
To give his music over to qualms
Of a sort the gods gaze in awe at . . .

(Gjertrud Schnackenberg, *The Throne of Labdacus*)

My heart is a poured-out bucket . . .

(Álvaro de Campos, alias Fernando Pessoa,
"The Tobacco Shop")

I shall never forget the sight of George Rochberg sitting in
front of the classroom, thrashing his arms through the air as he
sang the last movement of Beethoven's Seventh Symphony. Yes, I
do mean he *sang* it. No recording, no score — just Rochberg and
his visceral howl, which was truly terrifying, a hybrid of a chant
and a scream. Nor can I ever erase the image of Richard Wernick
staring at the score of Brahms's *German Requiem*, unable to
say anything, his gaze liable to burn a hole through the page.
Likewise fixed in my memory is the way George Crumb would
speak about Chopin's *Fantasy in F Minor* — under his breath,
like an oracle, surprising us all into rapt silence, instilling in us
not respect for the music, or even love, so much as *fear*. These
three were the Ancient Mariners of my own youth, stopping me
on my way to the feast, making me listen to their uncanny tales.
To put it another way, these events in my education felt to me
like theatre. They were a drama I could barely comprehend — as
if I were watching Sophocles performed in Greek. I had listened
to Beethoven's Seventh many times before; but when I watched
Rochberg "perform" the music, I was shocked into the realization that I had had no clue at all about the real character of the
piece, which possessed Rochberg like a demon. No, that's not
quite right: it was as if Rochberg was performing an exorcism

on the music, shaking the demon out so that we could see it and hear it roar. In my years at Penn, I had many occasions to hear comparable testimony from Wernick and Crumb.

Your song, what does it know? Celan's question seems to suggest that no song — no poem, or art of any kind — could ever properly address the depth of human suffering which reaches a climax in the enormity of the Holocaust he happened to survive. The *uncanniness* of my teachers' reckoning of Beethoven in particular strikes me now as a counterpoint to Celan's question. To Rochberg, Wernick, and Crumb, Beethoven looms so large because his song knows *too much*; it *kens* (the Scottish root for "uncanny"), to the extent that any performance of it — whether by an orchestra or by a professor waving his arms about, howling at the top of his lungs — must fall far short of what it knows. All essential readings of Beethoven, including Rochberg's wild song, are *uncanny* because they dare to grasp at a music that will always run ahead of them.

> . . . *For beauty is nothing*
> *but the beginning of terror, which we can still barely endure,*
> *and while we stand in wonder it coolly disdains*
> *to destroy us. Every Angel is terrifying.*

(Rainer Maria Rilke, *First Duino Elegy*,
translated by Edward Snow)

The opening octaves of the *Egmont Overture*, the pulsing theme of the Violin Concerto, the dissonant climax of the "Eroica" Symphony's first movement, and especially the first notes of the Fifth Symphony — these are all angelic tigers we have recklessly tried to tame. They would devour us in a minute if we entered the cage we have put them in. Having been devoured, we might begin to be whole again. If we gave these familiar items just a moment's reflection, they would make a mockery of all our efforts to turn them into clichés.

The famous pieces just cited all come from the same heroic decade of Beethoven's life. But early or late — from the opus 1 piano trios to the opus 135 string quartet — one abiding task he sets for himself (among other, more genial ones) seems very close to the task Gjertrud Schnackenberg assigns to the god of music: "to register cataclysm in a single pitch" (by coincidence, all of the themes mentioned feature held or repeated notes). In such passages, *the beauty of the music coincides with the terror of it.* It is this coincidence — between the radiance of great music and the demonic darkness that attends it — that makes the hapless narrator of Thomas Mann's *Doktor Faustus* feel so much disquiet at listening to Beethoven.

Why should there be so strong a connection between musical genius and the sinister sphere that Mann calls the *dæmonic*? (The addition to the word of the diphthong, henceforth permanent, will become part of the answer.) What earthly good can come from taking possession of something most music lovers are perfectly content not to recognize — that is, the *fearfulness* of great music? I do not know how to answer this question directly; but I hope you will stick with me as I approach it through a dark side-door.

In the dæmonic realm, there is always a certain void that lies beyond explanation. I want to confront that inexplicability, though I know I can never make peace with it. I want to confront the fury in Osama bin Laden's or Kim Jong-il's eye, in the way he carries himself, in the all-encompassing totalization of his own beliefs, which defeat rationality, even as they follow their own implacable logic. His hatred kills our scrutiny, even as it takes us in with its gaze. It unleashes a terror similar to seeing those films of Hitler or Stalin addressing their adoring masses, and a similar awe at the historical consequences of such insanity.

Something else scares me, too: I have an inkling that the feeling I have in these encounters with evil is the shameful brother to what I feel when I experience musical ecstasy. In both cases, I am aware of the most powerful configurations of pure feeling itself. No reason can be given for it. It is something that demands either complete capitulation or complete revulsion. It gives no quarter. Through such a reckoning, it is less difficult to understand how the Ninth could be so effectively exploited as the anthem of the Third Reich.

An immediate distinction must be made: music, even of the dæmonic sort, does not manufacture the violent deaths of innocent people. Celan's poem wonders if music can even *know* about such horrible things. My teachers taught me that music — Beethoven's, especially — knows *so* well about such things that the knowledge baffles and inspires in equal measure, making Beethoven's countless fans the natural, if unwitting, allies of all those — for example, Rochberg, Crumb, and Wernick — who reach uncompromisingly for the same "endarkenment."

The burden of knowing: this is what deathless music has to bear. It gives us the knowledge as a gift and lightens our load through all the various occasions inventoried in Ecclesiastes: "There is a time for weeping and a time for laughing, a time for wailing and a time for dancing." If music can sometimes belie historical truth by helping us to bear what is truly unbearable — and here is where the uncanny *harmoniousness* of Beethoven's music separates him conclusively from his more discordant progeny — it can also lend us a strange comfort in feeling close for a while "to that nether realm where we store our shadows, as if for future use" (a lovely comment by critic Geoffrey O'Brien on Alfred Hitchcock).

The Greek root of "demon" — of "dæmon," rather — provides a rounder image of the power of music. A *daimon* in Greek is a spirit who attends you and opens your mind to the strange and the new. It guides your actions and tempers your thought. A *daimon* is not just a fair-weather friend: it holds your hand all the more tightly when you enter the tract of darkness where the dæmonic awaits you, as strong as love, as sure as death. Beethoven the *daimon* whispered constantly in my teachers' ears. Hopeful, fearful, and amazed, I am coming to understand what that feels like on my own troubled and singing ground.

Chapter 6

Letting Go

We are mortal, balanced on a day, now and then
It makes sense to say Save what you can.

(Anne Carson, *The Beauty of the Husband*)

To live in this world

you must be able
to do three things:
to love what is mortal;
to hold it

against your bones knowing
your own life depends on it;
and, when the time comes to let it go,
to let it go.

(Mary Oliver, "In Blackwater Woods")

No, I am only trying to teach you
What pleasure is, and also about
The end of things,
And how the two of them go hand in hand.

(Howard Moss, "The Gallery Walk: Art and Nature")

I. LIZ THROWS A PARTY

At the start of twelfth grade, my high school administration released specific rankings to the top 50 students in our class, in order to inspire in us a healthy spirit of academic competition. I was second in the class and Liz Kelly was number one. That was all right with me because I was in love with her. Everyone was in love with her, especially us boys. My friend Herb cut out Liz's eleventh grade photo from the yearbook and carried it in his wallet. My best friend Matt was her boyfriend for a while, but when they broke up, he gave me his blessing to ask Liz out on a date. We went to the largest shopping mall in the United States (at the time), a 20-minute ride from our neighborhood, and wandered past all the shops, talking and laughing. I had never been so happy in all my life, and I could tell that she was happy, too. She always seemed a little sad, but she had a beautiful laugh, a lot like her Aunt Grace's, crystalline and warm. But Liz's laughter also had a quality of self-effacement, in harmony with her slouching posture, which she sweetly assumed for the boys she dated, for she was taller than any of us.

Liz was so smart, so eager to talk about books and movies and music. For my sixteenth and seventeenth birthdays, she got me Shakespeare's sonnets and *Robinson Crusoe*. But her greatest gift to me was Bruce Springsteen. The album *Born to Run* had come out in August of 1975 and certain songs on the album — including the eponymous one — remained the most popular anthems for my high school class through the fall of 1976. I'd heard "Born to Run" on the radio, but I was a Cat Stevens kind of guy, so the Boss seemed a bit rough around the edges to me. But I trusted Liz, simply because I loved her. It wasn't so much desire that motivated this love. Other girls were more adorable in that way. I just thought she was aces.

On the drive home from the mall, Liz invited me to a party at her house the following weekend. I said yes, mostly because I really wanted to see what the inside of the Kelly mansion looked like (the template for *The Philadelphia Story*, as well as for Aunt Grace's turn in *High Society*). Next weekend arrived on time, but I arrived late at the party, as the child of an overworked physician always does. The party was in full swing, most kids already high on Tab caffeine (Mrs. Kelly was a very responsible hostess). Liz was dancing with no one in particular — or rather, with everyone in the room. The song playing was (naturally) "Born to Run." We all have certain songs that get wrapped up with certain moments in our lives, staying forever associated with that time and place. Such songs constitute a very particular, personal species of the *audible sign*, incontrovertible proof that such signs exist at the individual level, which a handful of composers have the genius to lift up to the cultural level. This moment at Liz's party revealed to me — though I only understood it later — the dramatic capacity of a song to transcend its private effect on the listener and speak for an entire generation.

As I watched Liz dance to Springsteen, I also realized — once again, without any need for language to articulate the thought — that a particular person in a particular situation might be in a position to project the heart and soul of a song in all its timeless power, lyrical significance, and cultural impact. I had never seen Liz dance before. She was wild, all her self-effacement gone, her slouch replaced by an absolute physical confidence, her blazing intellect now channeled into raw, uninhibited feeling. She sang Bruce's lyrics as she danced, and I somehow knew — or at least took ineffable note of the fact so that I could consider it later — that even though the song narrated the flight of two kids from blue-collar hell and Liz Kelly belonged to the first family of Philadelphia high society, this was *her* story also, all about *her* need to break out, to cut loose, to get free, before her heart got broke.

The E Street Band roars down the opening instrumental refrain like a shower of sparks. The great leaping motto of the song grabs the listener by the collar (blue or white) and pulls him, pulls her, pulls Bruce and his sweet Wendy, right out of the rut they find themselves in, whether it's in the infernal oil refineries of New Jersey or the well-mannered lawns of the Main Line. Bruce's voice makes a compact ascent through each verse, drawn onto the graph of his growing self-awareness (a beautiful analogy to Paul's vocal odyssey in "Hey Jude"). At first we hear Bruce's singing as a muttering snarl of despair, but it rises, rises in sheer recklessness to a wavering pair of notes, held fast against a falling bass — so brave and precarious in its sustained height that the last thing we expect is the very thing that happens: a *further* ascent, unleashing the shout "WHOA-OA" at its peak. So sure is Bruce of his trajectory that now he can ride the crest of that wave of song. Then, with sudden parabolic logic, he falls back down to where he started. But this lower region of his voice, which was at first cursed with disaffection, now radiates with the energy released by his "WHOA-OA": he careens, he sidles, he slides right into his new consciousness, his birthright, the only inheritance that matters to those who are dispossessed, whether you are one of the "tramps like us" or a Philadelphia heiress: *baby, we were born to run.*

The process repeats, the second wave darker and scarier than the first, with more at stake because the road out is now in view, but not yet taken. Even at this point, after two completed verses, the breakthrough is only provisional, *not yet earned.* And so the bridge of the song begins its crucial work, laying down, plank by syncopated plank, the way over an interstate of doubt and inertia. The rhythmic hook of the song works overtime, like a factory, like a rolling millstone by a torrential spring (a *springsteen*, in Dutch). The ordeal hones the singer's spirit, sending him through a refiner's fire. But then the voice falls silent and the instruments collapse all in a heap, out of chromatic fury into rhythmic blankness. Out of this chaos of aural and spiritual equivocation, Bruce rallies himself and his fallen angels once more — once more unto the breach, dear friends, 1-2-3-4, the wild count launching a vast and vanquishing counterpoint, the recitative of the voice now joined to the ecstatic motto of the band, every bit of it earned by the sweat of the song's brow, a release of joy, freedom, heroic love, and terrible responsibility. We cannot know what will happen to this runaway boy and his Wendy after they make their escape. Their prospects cannot be very hopeful. But at this moment, we are with Bruce and Wendy all the way. The song enacts their liberation, exhilarating and terrifying in equal measure.

I witnessed this drama in real time that night watching Liz dance, stunned by my first encounter with an absolute communion between music and music lover. A sign was given to me of the awesome force music may possess under the right circumstances to transform a person into *who she authentically is*. But I also found myself face to face with a corollary truth, in the shape of a painful, Schumann-haunted question: how is a body supposed to make this self-possession *stick* when the music stops? What is she supposed to do when the song is over, apart from catching her breath and grabbing a Tab? Are we really only "the music while the music lasts"? I have always disliked this scrap of verse from the *Four Quartets*, mainly for its terrible truth-telling, but also for its typical Eliotic air of celebrating every other sphere of human activity except the most important one: tangible, frangible love, which Eliot wot not of.

My friend Liz was battling inherited demons I could never understand in my own happy youth. Springsteen was her comrade in arms — as I never could be — and so bright was his light for her in "Born to Run" that it utterly burned out when the music stopped. So did Liz that year. She dropped from valedictorian to the second spot in the class, and then altogether out of the top 50. She took up with a different crowd and much rougher music. I lost touch with her for the rest of high school. Years after we graduated, I used to drop in to say hello and purchase a fabulous treat at her pastry shop in center-city Philadelphia, slyly named Brickworks after her family's lost fortune. That soon closed and I heard from friends that she had taken the accidental death of her famous aunt very hard (the two of them had been close).

Last year, at an impromptu reunion of a few pals, my friend Brad (who wound up number two in the class after me) casually mentioned that Liz had died. With an instantaneous shock of cruelty, Springsteen's great song whooshed into my head, the band's crashing first chords saturating my inward ear, in untimely affirmation of all the things my beautiful friend had danced to so very long ago, while the music lasted.

"Born to Run" is a life wish raised against a death trap. Bruce and Wendy *let go* of everything pressing them down, holding them back, and they break through, their song bound as firmly to freedom as the two lovers are to each other, on the seat of their motorcycle. But what good is the song if so many who love it and live by it cannot find a way to realize its dream? This is the *offense of art* I refuse to let off the hook, the irresponsible ways in which art pretends to address suffering, while finally leaving the sufferer in the dust, in the trenches, in the gas chamber.

I have borne faithful witness to Liz grasping at the dream, even fulfilling it in her dance at the party. It would not, after all, take a degree in psychology to explain why I am so determined to hear the finale of Schumann's Second at a party. But there will always be a risk when self-fulfillment comes by way of ecstasy. The problem shows up right in the root meaning of this word, *ecstasy*: when we are moved by music to go *beside ourselves* with joy (*ek-stasis*), what happens to the self that is left behind? I reckon that both Schumann and my friend Liz suffered from this divided self. The ecstatic experience of music had not the power to point either of them towards spiritual wholeness; indeed, it might even have exacerbated the malady. An infamous example of this likelihood is the horrible perversion of Beethoven's Ninth in Anthony Burgess's *A Clockwork Orange*.

One bit of wisdom of rock 'n' roll music is never to judge a song — or a human being — by its cover, but to research the original version. Even better is not to judge at all, just to love. Springsteen's "Born to Run" enacts this difficult virtue and demands it from the listener. Bruce plays Orpheus to us stolid trees, moving us to uproot and dance.

All these things are Liz Kelly's gifts to me. I have turned around to glimpse her one more time. Now I let her go.

II. TO HELL WITH ORCUS

My friend BW has worked on both sides of the musical tracks. A student of the celebrated oboist John Mack, she has held positions in major orchestras, astonishing concert audiences with the preternatural purity of her playing. BW is also one of the best singer-songwriters of her generation, inspiring a devoted following wherever the winds of her stormy life have blown her. Her own songs illuminate the genius of the blues with the rich colors of classical music. Her best lyrics are about loss and recovery, charting the dark arc of her own experience with hard-earned clarity. It's no wonder record producers have had a hard time figuring out how to pitch her.

BW distrusts the intellect because she has seen too often how the thinking mind can smother the feeling heart. She makes close friends of academics, both because she likes us and because she likes to loiter in our groves, with the subversive intent of undermining our intellectual certainties. She is a born ironist: her intelligent argument for an amicable divorce between feeling and intellect is itself the most beautiful affirmation of their wedding vows.

After 11 years of playing in the Nashville Symphony and Music Row recording sessions and struggling to break into

the songwriting biz, BW left Nashville. I miss her a lot. I can
longer dispute the philosophy of music with her on a daily basis
(or a deli basis, for we would sometimes argue over pastrami
sandwiches). I recently attended a lecture-performance by a
songwriter in Nashville. At one point, he said that he writes songs
"from the neck down," to make sure his head doesn't get in the
way. The whole time he was talking, I was wishing BW could be
there with me, so she could help me bite his head off, to show
him exactly how effective a songwriter he would be if he had to
write a song from the neck down. BW may believe that the heart
is at war with the mind; but she knows that the main point is that
it is a war, in which the heart draws strength and courage from
the battle and cannot do without this militant energy.

Through her own example, BW has helped me to see that
feeling arises most intensely from the intellect's apprehension of
things. In the Hebrew language, there is but a single word, *lev*,
for "heart-at-one-with-mind":

> And you shall love the Lord your God with all your
> heart-mind [levav'cha], all your soul, and all your might.

A treasured moment from early in our friendship was the
time BW played through orchestral oboe excerpts for me, just
for the fun of it. When she got to the solo at the beginning of the
slow movement of the Brahms Violin Concerto, I knew that I
would never again hear this sweet melody rendered as beautiful
as she now played it. I think this recollection is such a potent one
because it involves Brahms, who, to my *lev*, consecrates over and
over again the union of heart and mind. I dedicate the following
investigation of Brahms, with love and gratitude, to BW.

Johannes Brahms has always held a privileged place in my
imagination, first because my mentors — who loved him so well
— gave him into my charge, and second because he has been
so strangely unloved by my academic colleagues and students.
The "experts" condemn Brahms's instrumental music for being

poorly realized enlargements of his art songs. These detractors define Brahms essentially by his *Lieder* and will not admit the possibility that his orchestral music (for instance) works as a quixotic transformation of symphony into song (hooray for Schumann's "corruption" of his protégé Brahms!). A majority of my composition students would rather listen to Brahms's songs than his symphonies, and for pretty much the same reason (also, because they are used to listening to songs).

Naturally, I am getting into Brahms by way of disputation, even though it should be obvious that Brahms needs no defense from me. His symphonies remain the bread and butter of symphony concert programs — one reason why it is such a struggle for living composers to get onto the bill. But if more folks could hear just how disconcerting (dis-*concert*-ing) Brahms's music really is, then they might be more inclined to take on the challenge of listening to the strange music my hopeful peers and I are cooking up right now, with the *daimon* Brahms whispering in our ears.

To confront — and thus dismantle — the alternately over-analyzed or naïve contempt for Brahms I have described above, let's dive into a short work called *Nänie* (Song of Lamentation). It is one of a handful of works in which Brahms does the very thing his detractors blame him for doing: he enlarges his song composition onto the grandest scale, replacing solo voice and piano accompaniment with full chorus and orchestra. My goal here is to "change the key" of Brahms criticism from

He turns symphonies into songs?! Yicch! boooo! hiss!

into

He turns symphonies into songs!! Yeehaa! woooo! hurrah!

An anxiety of influence thrills through *Nänie*, most tellingly in his choice of poet: it's Schiller, the same fellow who penned

Beethoven's "Ode to Joy." But this is an altogether different Schiller, here composing a lament in grand Homeric hexameters instead of the beer-garden tetrameters of the Ode. The presence of Homer's meter serves well the poem's imagery, culminating in the goddess Thetis's ascent from the sea to weep for the death of her great son Achilles. Brahms thus goes to *greater lengths* than Beethoven in taking on Schiller, both in the expanded length of "Nänie"'s poetic line and the epic scope of its content.

> *The beautiful, too, must die! That which subjugates men and*
>   *gods*
> *does not stir the brazen heart of the stygian Zeus.*
> *Only once did love melt the Lord of Shadows,*
> *and just at the threshold, he strictly yanked back his gift.*
> *Aphrodite does not heal the beautiful boy's wound,*
> *which the boar ripped cruelly in that delicate body.*
> *Neither does the immortal mother save the divine hero*
> *when, falling at the Scaean Gate, he fulfills his fate.*
> *She ascends from the sea with all the daughters of Nereus,*
> *and lifts up a lament for her glorious son.*
> *Behold! the gods weep; all the goddesses weep,*
> *that the beautiful perish, that perfection dies.*
> *But to be a dirge on the lips of loved ones can be a*
>   *marvelous thing;*
> *for that which is common goes down to Orcus in silence.*

As we discovered in Chapter 4, the texture of artistic innovation can be beautifully archaic ("barefoot," as I suggested). Three great breakthroughs of poetic imagination in the modern epoch — the invention of the operatic Baroque, the invention of Romanticism, and the invention of Modernism — hinged on the reinvention of Greek myth. When Schiller wrote this poem in 1799, he hoped to transform the sensibility of his modern readers by transporting them to the primal ground of our civilization's self-expression, when the dew of mythic creation was still wet on the earth and the tears of the goddess were still wet on her deathless cheek (so, too, in Monteverdi's *L'Orfeo*; so too, in James Joyce's *Ulysses*). To feel that beauty must die with all our hearts (Schiller implicitly argues) we must first thoughtfully *inhabit* the ancient myths of dying beauty.

I have purposely left out the explanatory footnotes that usually attend a translation of "Nänie" — not because I wish to withhold the information, nor merely to uphold my promise to you that there would be no footnotes in this book, but rather to emphasize what Schiller expects us to know without explanation. We can recognize Zeus and Aphrodite with relative ease; but what about "Scaean" or "Nereus," let alone the unnamed Orpheus and Adonis, and the central figure Thetis herself, all of whom are elliptically present in the poem? Just as Schumann expects us to recognize Mendelssohn, Bach, Beethoven, and Haydn in his symphony's finale, Schiller does not question our ability to identify his brief poem's rather long cast of characters. Are these Romantics asking too much of us? If we think so, are we expecting too little of ourselves?

One reason I love Brahms so much is because there exists in his music — as in my own life — a fine line between pomposity and enthusiasm. For Brahms, this line is precariously thin, on account of his fourfold belatedness: he is late after Schumann, he is quite late after Beethoven, he is awfully late after Schiller, and he is way too late after Homer, even the Romanticized one that comes to him through Schiller. How very late Brahms is — and feels himself to be — is clarified further when we examine the canvases of his friend Anselm Feuerbach, the painter whose death prompted Brahms to set Schiller's "Nänie" to music in 1881. Feuerbach was a neoclassicist whose old-fashioned imitations of Jacque-Louis David now look both pompous and pathetic. Whatever we might say about Brahms's conservative tastes in painting, he no doubt selected the Schiller text as a shrewd tribute to his classicizing friend. If Brahms felt himself to be late in a lyrical vein, he must have at least considered the problem of Feuerbach's more extreme belatedness as a painter, when Manet, Pissarro, Degas & Co. were already winning the artistic soul of Europe.

Feuerbach's paintings are all too *common* to the Victorian-era academic salon. Therefore, there is a good deal of ironic *pathos* in Brahms's setting of Schiller's closing line:

> *. . . for that which is common goes down to Orcus in silence.*

No, no, indeed not! In *this* case, that which is common becomes *marvelous*, becomes *a dirge on the lips of the loved one*! Brahms could not imagine that Feuerbach's artistic legacy would be so meager, nor do I think it would have mattered to him. The only thing that mattered to Brahms was to lament his dead friend, to lament dear Anselm with all his heart. Feuerbach becomes *uncommon* as a result of this song, not as painter but as beloved friend. Orcus — the darkest region of the underworld — cannot hold him any longer, at least not while Brahms rises, Thetis-like, out of his sea of tears to offer up this dirge.

Of all composers, Brahms summons up more than anyone for me the ancient Greek figure of speech, *aporia*. Even if we could listen to *Nänie* together in the same room, I would be so drowned by its torrent of exquisite sonorities and deathless truths that I would not know where to begin to tell you what I was experiencing. *Nänie* defeats all my rhetorical abilities, leaving me dumbstruck with awe and bewilderment. This is the condition called *aporia*. The aspect, above all, which induces this feeling of descriptive inadequacy is the matter BW and I have been arguing about all these years: the wedding of heart and mind, celebrated at every moment of Brahms's music. Far beyond his friend Feuerbach's capacity, even surpassing Schiller's art — for Schiller had no chorus or orchestra to aid him — Brahms crosses the constitutional divide from pomposity to enthusiasm — literally, "the god within."

The gods brandished so ponderously by Schiller — his poem

overcrowded with event, like Achilles' shield — are lightened by Brahms's music, starting on BW's own sweet instrument: a valediction in the oboe, a recognizable quotation of the opening motto of Beethoven's "Farewell" Piano Sonata ("Das Lebewohl," Op. 81a). Brahms expects us to recognize the Beethoven, just as he expects us to know who fell at the Scaean Gate (as well as where in the world *that* was); but in Brahms, much less depends upon such knowledge than in either Schiller or Schumann. Brahms's saturating tunefulness makes the presence of his heroes — both referenced gods and quoted composers — at once more subtle *and* supererogatory (there's that wonderful word again, whose sesquipedalian splendor fulfills its sense of "excessive generosity").

Brahms's setting of "Nänie" performs the miracle of all great commentaries (Rashi on Torah, Huxley on Darwin, Kenner on Joyce): *towards their sources, they shed a clarifying light and dispense a complicating thought.* How does Brahms *clarify* Schiller? That one's easy: while Schiller has need of discursive language — beginning with a thesis (*The beautiful, too, must die!*) and developing it through a string of didactic exemplifications — Brahms subsumes Schiller's discourse to lyrical outpouring from the outset. Schiller does not really sing at all at first; rather, he *orates* his elegiac theme. The poem arrives very belatedly at its obvious lyrical symbol of Thetis' ascent and lament, well past the halfway mark. In joyful compensation, Brahms sets right this poetic wrong, setting in motion both qualities of ascent and lament *immediately*, from the first phrases of his song. No Brahmsian belatedness on this score!

How does Brahms *complicate* Schiller? Well, that one's not so easy, for things get complicated. The music of Thetis' emergence from the sea — the "high-water mark" of the piece, as it were — turns out to be the *least* lyrical passage of "Nänie":

> She ascends from the sea with all the daughters of Nereus,
> and lifts up a lament for her glorious son.

These lines are sung in grandiose heroic mode, verging on the pompous. The chorus and orchestra come close here to sounding like what Feuerbach's paintings look like — a peculiarly artificial extension of the composer's longing for his lost friend. But this overwrought grandeur is all part of Brahms's plan, forcing us to think through the myth of divine mother and mortal son as an objective, heroic, *exterior* event of our common mythology (*Behold! the gods weep; all the goddesses weep, that the beautiful perish, that perfection dies*). Once we have made this reckoning, we may at last take up our grief as a subjective, lyrical, *interior* burden, both lightened and enlightened by myth.

At last, the supreme moment of Schiller's insight arrives: humanity's imperfect forms of grieving unite with those of the gods, who are equally hapless in the face of death. The gods must take their lament onto mortal ground — or rather, sea, upon which Thetis must weep for her son like any mortal mother. Brahms makes manifest this "reverse apotheosis" — this elevation of human grief, to which even the gods must submit — as a stunning *structural* fulfillment. The first oboe melody recapitulates, opening once more the floodgates of lyricism. What was simple in the music at the start of the piece now becomes deliberately *simplistic*, the choral parts transparent as never before. The previous section ends with the mournful invocation, *Behold! the gods weep; all the goddesses weep, that the beautiful perish, that perfection dies*. But on that last word "dies" (*stirbt*) — as the chorus comes to rest on its final note — *the accompanying orchestra refuses to die!* It lands instead on a "deceptive cadence" (what a fabulous technical term from music theory!), immediately launching the imperishable oboe melody.

Brahms's orchestra repudiates Schiller's word "dies," just as Beethoven refuses to say goodbye in his "Farewell" Piano Sonata (listen for the opening deceptive cadence there, stolen by Brahms here). The whole of Schiller's discursive thought, the bulging catalogue of myths, the cold comfort that even the gods must weep — all these mindful measures of Schiller's elegy wind up at this moment of thwarted ending. What we thought was the absolute terminus turns into something else, something *further*. Brahms's would-be heroic cadence opens out into unending song, just as Schiller's 14 lines of would-be sonnet refuse at last to bend to any scheme but Homer's. The Romantic spirit — framed historically by Schiller and Brahms — takes the hard facts of Classicism and shapes them into an unanticipated lyricism. Thought and feeling merge in sacred communion, clarified and complicated through song.

Brahms's song, what does it know? What has it earned? The certain knowledge that *even to be a song of lamentation in the mouth of the beloved is splendid* (I like this alternate translation very much). As consolation, this is not much; but it is all the more precious for its modesty and realizable truth. Such poetic realism (the great legacy of Schiller, Goethe, Wordsworth, Keats, *et al.*) has rarely been acknowledged in popular conceptions of Romanticism, generally preoccupied with more obvious Romantic notions of vaunting heroism and supernatural striving. And yet, with great realism, Romantic heroes are invariably undone by their *hubris*. The lamentable Achilles and Prometheus are naturally mythic templates in this regard.

This spiritual frankness of the Romantics has exerted a potent revolution on the minds and hearts of the West, holding up the strange, agnostic assertion that Christian optimism is the enemy of real hope. Schiller and Brahms both proclaim: *To hell with Orcus* (no apologies for the redundancy). Still more subversively, their works are always crying out, *To hell with heaven!* We need not seek beyond Schiller's starry canopy, where, after all, *only* a loving Father *might* dwell. For it is here, and only here, in this mortal sphere (the iconoclastic ground of Brahms's *German Requiem*), where we can count on something truly splendid, if not necessarily divine: we can count on each other to sing while we are alive together, and also when we are gone. What else should we hope for? Every other blessed thing is already in our possession, when we have been vouchsafed *this* truth. Eternity

cannot hold a candle to it; burning candles are as mortal as
human lives.

In defiance of Schiller, Brahms brings his song to rest at the
end of the poem's *penultimate* line instead of its actual ending
(recall that Beethoven takes similar liberties with Schiller's Ode).
Brahms lets Schiller's best word linger and resonate through the
final cadence, releasing all its fine ambiguity: *herrlich* — splendid, marvelous if you will, or even godlike, for *Herr* can be used
in German to address God. *To be a song of lamentation in the
mouth of the beloved . . . that is splendid, marvelous, godlike.* Is
this conclusion really consoling for the death of a loved one? I
don't know. What I do know is that consolation is not all we need
to face the task of grieving. We need a breakthrough. Brahms's
Nänie does not merely console, it *breaks through* grief, offering no sops of comfort to the bereaved, but instead one single,
simple, fragile piece of reality:

> *If you sing, and sing with deathless beauty,*
> *your lost loved one becomes marvelous.*
> *That's it, that's all you can do.*
> *Now do it, whatever "singing" may be for you.*
> *And when the time comes to let it go,*
> *let it go.*

Mary Oliver may not approve this adaptation of the final lines
of her great poem "In Blackwater Woods" (one of the epigraphs
at the start of this chapter); but I have set three of her poems to
music, including this one, with her permission, so I trust she will
forgive me. I take her at her word (but one).

My father died of cancer in 1988, the same year Robert
Shaw's recording of *Nänie* appeared, with the Atlanta Symphony
Orchestra and Chorus (this superb CD includes other short
works by Brahms for chorus and orchestra). I gave the disc to
my mother a few weeks after the funeral. She was in bad shape.
I didn't know if Brahms could help. Even now, more than two

decades later, I can't say if it did "help," in any reasonable sense of the word. All I know is that my mom played the disc over and over again, all through that first year of her irrevocable loss. I could hear *Nänie* in the background while we talked on the phone. Oddly enough, the other music that got her through those dark months was Wagner's Overture to *Rienzi*, one of the most pompous pieces of Romantic orchestral music. Just as there is no accounting for Brahms's taste for Feuerbach's art, there is no accounting for my mother's taste for Brahms and Wagner as her unlikely allies in grief. We human beings can be stupid, self-deceiving, self-destructive in our ways of dealing with loss; or we can be splendid, marvelous, *herrlich*. My mother heard something common to both *Nänie* and *Rienzi* that made them uncommonly good company for her in her mourning. The act of listening to them again and again became a steady, sustained act of letting go of her husband. Let me be more precise, or, rather, more complex: my mother could better hold onto my dead father by letting her grief go out into the music. She grieved *into* Wagner's pompous overture, *right into* Brahms's enthusiastic lament, and my dad suffered his sea change, turning rich and strange through their singing. *Those are pearls that were his eyes.* Thanks to Shakespeare, to Schiller, to Brahms, to Springsteen, even to Wagner, to countless other allies, including both Testaments, we are *human* in our loss, not swine; we seize the pearls of irremediable grief cast before us.

Chapter 7

A Letter to My Daughter

Dear Maggie,

I am writing this to share with you one of *my favorite things*. And just like the scene where that song comes in *The Sound of Music*, these notes will move back and forth between the brightness of my favorite thing and the stormy darkness it holds at bay.

After Mom, you, your little brother Izzy, Grandma Ryda, Nene, all our family and friends, and our sweet dog Yofi, the things I care most about are these: music, poems, Old Master drawings and rocks. I list them here not in the order of their importance to me, but rather according to how much time I spend with each of them. You know better than anyone how much time that is, for it is time I have not spent with you. I am writing this partly to try to give back to you some of that time, or at least to offer some of its fruits to you. There may be a few thorns, too; but none that can draw blood, I promise.

. . . *draw blood* . . . there's the verb drawing me to share a favorite drawing with you. Let's find out where it draws us, and how it might draw us together:

***God's Promise to Abraham* by Rembrandt**

When I look at a drawing, Maggie, whether it's a good one or a bad one — or a great one, like this — what immediately gets to me is the feeling in it. I long considered this attitude of looking to be an inferior default mode, necessitated by my lack of knowledge about how drawings were actually made (their *technique*, that is). Naturally I would focus on what I felt when looking at one, since I had no inkling of how the artist drew it.

I came to understand that this distinction between feeling and technique is not real. I know loads about musical technique (maybe too much), but it is still the feeling that gets to me right away when I hear a piece of music. It has only taken me my whole life to grasp a simple truth: *we feel the most when we make things*. The things we make become the living sites of our feelings. The better we can make things — the finer the technique we are able to wield in their making — the more life our feelings will have in them. It turns out that in concentrating on what I was feeling when looking at a drawing, I was already involved with how the artist made it, even if I did not have the technical vocabulary to describe the work's manufacture (ink, crayon, charcoal, bister, graphite, wash, watercolor, gouache, pastel).

The unity of technique and feeling holds for all the things I love: music, poems, drawings — and yes, even rocks. I know it's crazy, but I believe that the earth's experience of geological transformation — so visible in rocks — is just that: an *experience*, something undergone, a passage through time and change, under tremendous pressure, or heat, or age-long consolidation. These are the earth's techniques for rock formation, not *designed* (for God's sake, no!), but rather *designated* by exigent, physical reality. Is it going too far to say that the Earth *feels* all of this? Is it absurd to propose that a rock — whether a piece of Dartmoor granite or a chunk of Nashville limestone — is the spontaneous, technical product of all that feeling? Perhaps; but there is a scientific theory supporting the notion, the Gaia theory, whose evidence for a living organism called Planet Earth grows steadily every year, with urgent warning, with urgent warming.

Science offers proofs for the living rock. Religion fortunately offers no such proofs — only truths, which can be understood (in widely divergent ways) only if they can be *interpreted* through an intelligent combination of faith and doubt. Consider what the Book of Genesis has in mind, how we can put its unhistorical truths to best possible use. God creates *Adam* from the Earth (*adamah*). God — who is sometimes invoked in Hebrew as a rock (*tzur*) — makes the human (*humus*, Earth) in His own image, a rock shaped into life, the product of divine feeling, a passage undergone through age-long time and change — six days and a billion years.

Now let's look at Rembrandt's drawing, *God's Promise to Abraham*. There God stands — or rather leans, supported on either side by two smaller figures (angels?), a pair of wings hovering over His head, a chaos of shapes and forms trailing behind Him. So much force is unleashed by his arrival, so much movement and presence! But that's not where the feeling of the drawing lies. It lies spread out on the ground, right there along the length of the floor, in Abraham, who thrusts himself back towards the earth, biting the dust from which his ancestor Adam was formed by this very Being who now appears in a human space for the first time, overwhelming humanity with His covenant.

The apparition of God commands awe, but Abraham *embodies* it. See how his right hand struggles to hide the awful sight from his eyes, which — though we cannot see them — must be tightly shut in terror? See how his bare toes push against the hard floor, as if they would go through and under and be gone from this fearful place? Abraham's staff lies there also, its usefulness gone, but it is pointed towards us, implicating us in the scene ("to implicate" means *to fold into*, like your grandmother's origami). The Torah almost never tells us what its characters are feeling (Sarah's laughter is one terrific, if still ambiguous, exception); in Rembrandt, it becomes startlingly clear that the only thing that matters in the Bible is what the characters are feeling.

The suddenness of Abraham's predicament is what terrifies me the most, Maggie. This vision comes to him not out of the blue, but out of the wall. In an instant, he confronts a concrete reality that cannot possibly be gotten around, and it knocks him flat. Have we ever had such overwhelming proof of our own unworthiness? Have we ever suffered such puniness in the face of such grandeur? We must have done, for we grasp it here imme-diately, without hesitation. Abraham's heartbreaking mortality, his beautiful, hidden face, his recognizable *personhood* — these are the treasures of Rembrandt's drawing, reflecting the fact that an accurate reckoning of the human being is the paradoxical treasure of all great transcendent religions.

Embodies — isn't that a wonderful word? Something as real as Abraham's prostrate body is turned into a *feeling* by the artist, who *em*-s the *body* with his art. A drawing is made from real ink on real paper, both having grown in the first place out of real earth. The lines are then transformed by the artist's *idea* into something even more real: into life itself. The story of Adam's creation happens over and over again, in countless drawings.

Let's get back to the drawing's God. I have a particular question for you about Him. I know you like observational comedy, and I believe the question has a touch of that kind of ironic humor. Why do you think Rembrandt shows us an image of a human-looking God — a beautiful, vulnerable, almost feminine-looking God — right at the very moment when He arrives to help Abraham overturn idolatrous images of gods?

There may be a clue in the statue visible in the background, which I take to be one of the idols Abraham means to overturn. The statue is rigid in shape, faceless in figure, literally *a bust*, without human feeling or interest, set squarely on its platform, locked into its appointed niche. The difference between that lifeless icon in the background and the bursting image of God in the foreground could not be greater. Everything about the figure of God breaks the statue's mold. No geometry can hold God in place, no earthly niche can contain Him; he swoops into the room with light and wind and cloud in His wake, so that there could be no more effective destruction of the old, inert simulacrum than to set this new, roaring reality in plain contrast to it.

What I think we must always keep in mind is that the artist only has the *visible* to work with. If Rembrandt were a poet or composer, he could have given us a new song, so we could *hear* just how completely the world has changed, now that God has arrived to make this covenant with Abraham (that's what the psalms do). As things stand, Rembrandt has no choice but to *show* us what this transformation looks like. I know it's contradictory, but the only way the artist has to overthrow the notion of imaging God is through an image.

Now we are ready to ask the next question: why does an all-powerful God need to be held up by two helpers, one on either side? Maybe because it is all wrong for him to be here in the first place, in this world of images — the world of His Creation, but not of his own Being, which transcends image. It is as if earth's gravity and atmosphere were too much for Him, and instead of a spacesuit and air boosters, He has brought along a headpiece of wings and a couple of sturdy angels.

It is all wrong for God to be here, but He comes in any case — to assure His chosen and beloved servant of their shared purpose, and to do so on Abraham's own ground, in such a way that the poor man can comprehend what has happened, even as it knocks him flat with terror. God shows up, finally, just to *be* here — right here, face to face, not anywhere else, certainly not in that dark recess of the statue's niche.

This image of God touches the limits of image-making by showing how inadequate images are. Artists have been trying to do the same thing ever since, but never again with the same thrill of inaugurating a new idea about what art can do. The very best way to inaugurate a new idea about what art can do is to focus on the problem of what it *cannot* do (to show God, for one thing). This is the never-before-seen, self-contradictory power of Rembrandt's art and influence.

I am a composer, Maggie, a professional musician. So why, in God's name (!), am I writing to you about a drawing? Like it or not — I don't like it much, either! — I'm a role model for you, and I guess I want to complicate that fact, so that you will never be quite sure which role of mine you may be modeling, or adapting, or opposing, or — Abraham-like — knocking off its stupid pedestal. You and I both love Stephen Sondheim's great show, *Into the Woods*, where the witch — after losing her daughter Rapunzel in the second-act tragedy that overturns the comedy of act one — sings, "Careful the things you say, children will listen. Careful the things you do, children will see. And learn." Bernadette Peters sings this so beautifully, overwhelming us with the realization that all her craft, all her protective sorcery, are for naught, for they could not save her daughter. Your mother and I do not want to be in control of you — locking you in a tower, your long hair hanging dangerously out the window — in order to love you. I am being careful here, to show you — and to affirm for myself

— that *you do not have to be an expert about something in order to love it.* Just as you do not have to be a musician — in control of a technical vocabulary — to talk intelligently about music, you do not have to be an art historian to write intelligently about art. That's what I am hoping to show you with this drawing.

All you need to flourish and have fun in the world is to develop and to share ideas, however strange they may be — not *opinions*, but *ideas* — and, furthermore, to found them upon vivid evidence. I already know, to my cost, that you are ready to dispute *my* ideas. What I hope is that you will welcome such disputation as the springboard for civility and mutual understanding. I think you know this already — though perhaps "civility" and "mutual understanding" are not the most accurate terms to characterize our furious debates with each other, as ancient as Zeus and Athena, as risky as Lear and Cordelia.

As a final stroke of paternal chutzpah, I am going to turn my attention to your own favorite singer/songwriter, Regina Spektor. I know I'm on shaky ground here. Even though I am a composer and music professor, what could I possibly say to you about Regina that you don't already know? Once again, I insist on the principle that no expertise is required to have and to share ideas — only love. And I do love Regina's music, Maggie. Here's why.

In the song called "Us" (from *Soviet Kitsch*, 2004), Regina sums up everything I've been trying to say to you, and does it much more poetically. She sings a scathing critique of so-called *expertise*, the dire enemy of authentic selfhood and loving relation. The "experts" presume to tell us who we are and where we stand. Whether they are parents, teachers, or politicians, they all want to cram us into our identities, turn us into stone, and set us up as statues on a mountaintop. They even want to "name a city after us and later say it's all our fault." With one hand, the "experts" tell us who we are; with the other hand, *they blame us for being that.* As soon as they are finished defining us to ourselves and to everybody else, they turn against us:

> *then they'll give us a talking to*
> *Because they've got years of experience*

They want to rob us of our true selves, and they do it by setting up a false image of who we are. Although the song speaks of a timeless human predicament, its lyrics reflect Regina's first-hand experience in her Russian childhood of the psychological nightmare the Soviet Union perpetrated for decades upon its various subject populations. They *did* make statues of Lenin and Stalin, named cities after them, and it *was* all their fault. A gigantic statue of Stalin stood for many years atop a hill in Prague, where the Czech writer Milan Kundera would have seen it as the avatar of "Soviet kitsch" — the term he invented for all the bad art, poetry and music enlisted to propitiate the bloodthirsty gods.

"We're living in a den of thieves," sings Regina. She turns into a Hebrew prophet just like Amos or Hosea, crying hard truths right in the marketplace (i.e., iTunes), chanting over and over again, "and it's contagious, and it's contagious," this disease of stolen selfhood, this idolatry of false expectation and imposed identity. The world has always needed such prophets to knock false idols out of their niches. Regina is the best iconoclast I've heard in a long, long time. Just like Rembrandt's drawing, she gives us an ironic and divine image of image-wrecking. Her piano playing is an audible sign of this dangerous manual labor, the pulsing, staccato figure *obstinately* hammering out its reckless *ostinato* (in these two italicized words, you can hear the English cognate of the Italian term). Regina's anger and defiance grow with each verse. Like Paul McCartney and Bruce Springsteen, she knows that *a singer evolves through the act of singing; she earns the right to sing by doing the work of singing.* I don't know anyone singing nowadays who works harder than Regina Spektor, Maggie. Her voice flies apart like bird call, like shattered rock, often cutting across the syllables of a single word so that we can hear its inner tension and semantic multiplicity. She breaks open the word "contagious" like a geode, so that we can hear its internal crystals of meaning, "conta[in]" and "us," for that's what the "experts" try to do to us, Maggie: they do their worst to *contain us*, to "make us wear our scarves just like a noose," they set us up, those demons, just so they can knock us down in the end. I vow to you that I will never do that to you. I would rather die. Regina is your ally, and so am I. Your love for her music is contagious. Thank you for giving her to me. I want to do the same for the readers of this book: I want to give them the music I am writing about. Like any good iconoclast, you're a chip off the old block. That sure beats making a statue of us.

Afterword

Six individuals (among many others) have enabled me to write this book, though they are in no way responsible for its faults. Each has worked wonders in the world, delivering beautifully obdurate things as gifts of understanding, with all their difficulties intact. All six know how, in one stroke, to shed a clarifying light and dispense a complicating thought. They have devoted their lives to such alchemies of the heart. I shall name them in reverse alphabetical order.

Peter Sheppard Skærved happens to be the among the greatest living violinists, but like his heroes Paganini, Joachim, and Louis Krasner, he plies this artistic ascendancy as a function of a larger project to establish communities of musical collaboration and inquiry wherever he goes. As both player and thinker, Peter treats (for instance) the music of George Rochberg, Gloria Coates, and Sir Michael Tippett — three irreconcilable composers — with the same unifying fervor as he treats Bach, Beethoven, and Brahms — and who dares to call these three disparate B's "reconcilable"? Peter makes his listeners at once more grateful and more mindful of the access composers always give into their worlds, unconstrained by either historical distance or proximity. I have lately been angry at my friend Peter for not allowing me and my family to extend to him a Nashvillian welcome of the kind he and his family have bestowed upon us in London. This unseemly *animus* helps to explain the spirit of this book: in these pages, I unreasonably hope to give back, out of my meager hospitality, what I can never repay to the bestowers of my musical vocation, Peter Sheppard Skærved chief among them.

Bill Rosenthal, an expert on mathematics education, has given up secure and distinguished academic positions *twice*. His decision to cut loose was for a seemingly different reason in each case; but the same principle was always (or as Bill would say, "o-ways") at stake. For Bill, it is not enough to teach math, never enough merely to teach anything. The only reason we are on this planet is to provide to others out of our own resources the life-giving tools to provide to others out of their own resources the life-giving tools to provide to others out of their own resources . . . To my friend Mr. Bill, there is no such thing as mere knowledge or information; there is only the better life, the critical thinking, the political consciousness, which knowledge or information empowers. For most students, math is the most unlovable of subjects. Bill Rosenthal not only helps teachers to make math more lovable to students; he helps teachers to make students more lovable to themselves, through the study of math. He is able to work these miracles because he is possessed by that most elusive genius of all: *laughter*, which is all the more transformative in the face of vanquished despair. (Typical of our conversations are four homophonic aliases concocted for *Audible Signs*: *Audible Sighs*, *Edible Scions*, *Eight-Ball Science*, and *Oddball Zionists*.)

Ryda Rose is also an expert on education. She mentored several generations of graduate students through the Science Education Program at the University of Pennsylvania. For 30 years, her laboratory was famous at Penn for its surface chaos and its underlying order. She insisted on dramatizing to her students every day a principle her colleagues took too much for granted: the simple fact that to teach anything to children, you must master it yourself. Ryda *performed* her science for her disciples, peppering her pedagogy with crazy hats and awful show tunes. It is the prerogative of every mother to embarrass her son. In my case, my mother Ryda Rose embarrassed me right into my life's work.

A clarifying light and a complicating thought — these are terms very suitable to Brian H. Peterson's work. Brian is a photographer who loves the natural world with a breathtaking passion. His images of the earth and his self-portraits radiate an intelligence at once fearless of mortality (an empty abstraction) and fearful of death (an embodied fact). The same light shines through his work as museum curator and published author. *The Smile at the Heart of Things* is the title of Brian's most recent book. In it, he makes obvious several things that have never been properly understood, for they seem too good to be true. For example, my friend Brian makes the case that our defining character as human beings is our *hunger* for the universe we find ourselves in. I balked at this notion at first, strongly objecting to the word choice. I could not help feeling that *hunger* is so abjectly negative a term — an externally imposed, *physical* condition for many millions of people around the world — that it ought not to be so blithely converted into a *spiritual* term (though I am guilty of this usage myself a few times in this book). Brian and I argued about it for two hours over the phone, and then for another hour after I asked him to read this paragraph. He said that my scruples were veering dangerously close to political correctness and I said nanny nanny boo boo. Such are the respective levels of maturity in our disputations. I may not like Brian's overarching "hunger" idea, but it is doing its work on me, helping me to understand my need for cosmic connection. Thanks to his importuning wisdom, I can feel metaphorical bits of the universe adding every day to my fleshly avoirdupois, making me feel lighter by the minute. In my friendship with Brian Peterson, gravity always becomes grace.

My late friend and long-time pen pal Guy Davenport — essayist, classicist, modernist scholar, artist, teacher, and Calvinist pagan — gave conclusive evidence throughout his life and work that all harmony (aesthetic, social, or spiritual) is based on both *balance* and *distance*. Undue closeness, argued Guy, invariably leads to discord, meanness, and sentimental "wetness" — all failures of harmony, all opposed to the dictum of Heraclitus (one of the seven Greeks Guy famously translated), that "a dry light is the best soul." In the title essay of *The Geography of the Imagination* — the most harmonious book I have ever read — Guy's searing intellect burns through the occluding familiarity of a number of objects — the stories of Poe, the poems of Walt Whitman, Grant Wood's *American Gothic* — and reveals the intricate harmony at work and at play in them. Like my friend Peter Sheppard Skærved, Guy lavishes the same loving attention on obscure or academically unfashionable figures (Ronald Johnson, Charles Burchfield, O. Henry) as he does on canonical ones (Ezra Pound, Pablo Picasso, James Joyce), the only criterion being the balance they afford his labyrinthine imagination, the only principle being the exemplary manner in which they all realize the Shaker saying, "Every Force Evolves a Form" (the title of another of Guy's books of essays). At the start of our friendship in 1988, it took me many months to chip away at Guy's refusal to let me come see him in Lexington, Kentucky. I visited him and Bonnie Jean a half-dozen times over the years, dragging along girlfriends, wife, child, all to marvel at the sage of Sayre Avenue, who sat on his stored-up treasures of art and literature like a beneficent dragon, breathing Heraclitan fire at his fortunate guests. At the end of our friendship in 2004, it again took me many months to read between the lines of Guy's final letters and discover, too late, that he was dying of lung cancer. This dreadful, final coup of "harmonizing distance" which Guy enacted in our friendship was the most difficult lesson I have ever learned in my life — even more painful to me than my father's dying, which I gratefully attended. I still have not forgiven Guy, whatever that might mean posthumously. In the same way, I can never "forgive" Joyce or O. Henry, Picasso, or Burchfield, for being so drily distant from my wet and easy grasp. I am able to love these figures because of Guy, who took all things exceptionally unyielding to the human heart — poems, novels, paintings, death itself — and delivered them as gifts of ongoing understanding, with all their obdurate beauties intact.

Joanna Brichetto has surveyed the texts and ritual practices of that unwieldy organism called Judaism and has divined the secret of its implausible survival: a capacity to speak joyfully to children, who will then — because of all the fun they had at synagogue — grow up to have Jewish children of their own. Out of her boundless craftiness, Joanna has devised a set of strategies to draw kids (i.e., their parents) back to *shul* for *shabbos*, beating the rabbis at their own game. It's not enough to smear honey on a page of Hebrew letters, to make them taste sweet to children; you've got to bake whole honey cakes for the kids to eat, in the shapes of those ancient letters of Torah. So many American Jews have left Judaism, its wonders no longer nourishing to them, let alone sweet. Joanna restores these wonders to her fellow Jewish parents as gifts of understanding, with all their difficulties intact. She lets the children lead the way (well, that *is* the greatest love of all), for toddlers have no trouble enjoying the contradictory narratives of Eden or the Flood. She has unlocked for me the most obdurate thing in my own nature: a belated capacity to love things I have taken badly for granted, like my own faith tradition, like my own life. What I have owed to joy, I owe to her, in the company of our two children, Maggie and Izzy. This book is for Joanna Brichetto.

Suggestions for Further Listening, Viewing, and Reading

Here are the musical, visual, and literary works given particular focus or citation in *Audible Signs*, listed in order of appearance. Every one of them has delighted, enlightened, challenged, and/or infuriated me. I hope they will work as variously upon you:

Ross, Alex. *The Rest Is Noise: Listening to the Twentieth Century*. New York: Farrar, Straus and Giroux, 2007.

Michael Gelven. *The Asking Mystery: A Philosophical Inquiry*. University Park, PA: The Pennsylvania State University Press, 2000.

Caravaggio, Michelangelo Merisi da. *Maddelena penitente* (1594–1595). Rome, Galleria Doria Pamphilj. Permission information available on copyright page.

Focillon, Henri; translated by Hogan, Charles B. and Kubler, George. *The Life of Forms*. New York: Zone Books, 1989.

Sacks, Oliver. *Musicophilia: Tales of Music and the Brain* (revised and expanded). New York: Vintage Books, 2008.

Collins, Billy. *Sailing Alone Around the Room: New and Selected Poems*. New York: Random House, 2001.

Mozart, Wolfgang Amadeus. *Serenade for Winds in B-Flat Major*, K. 361, "Gran Partita" (1781); *Così fan tutte*, opera buffa (1790).

Forman, Miloš, director; Shaffer, Peter, writer. *Amadeus* (1984).

Mann, Thomas; translation by Lowe-Porter, H. T. (Helen Tracy). *Doctor Faustus: The Life of the German Composer Adrian Leverkühn, as Told by a Friend.* New York: Alfred A. Knopf, 1948.

Davenport, Guy. *The Geography of the Imagination: Forty Essays.* Jaffrey, NH: Nonpareil Books, 1997.

Merwin, W.S. *Migration: New and Selected Poems.* Port Townsend, Washington: Copper Canyon Press, 2005.

Vaughan Williams, Ralph. *Dona Nobis Pacem*: Cantata for Soprano, Baritone, Chorus, and Orchestra (1936).

Spielberg, Steven, director; Williams, John, composer. *Schindler's List* (1993).

Heaney, Seamus. *The Redress of Poetry.* New York: Farrar, Straus and Giroux, 1995.

Shakespeare, William. Sonnet VIII: "Music to hear, why hear'st thou music sadly?"

McCartney, Paul. "Hey Jude" (1968). Permission information available on copyright page.

Beethoven, Ludwig van. *Symphony No. 9 in D Minor*, opus 125 (1824).

Riley, Tim. *Tell Me Why: The Beatles: Album by Album, Song by Song, The Sixties and After.* Cambridge, MA: Da Capo Press, 2002.

Masser, Michael and Creed, Linda, writers; Whitney Houston, performer. "Greatest Love of All" (1986).

Riefenstahl, Leni, director. *The Triumph of the Will* (1934).

Levi, Primo; translated by Woolf, Stuart. *Survival in Auschwitz.* New York: Touchstone, 1996.

Bloom, Harold. *The Anxiety of Influence: A Theory of Poetry.* New York: Oxford University Press, 1997.

Quinney, Laura. *The Poetics of Disappointment: Wordsworth to Ashbery*. Charlottesville, VA: University of Virginia Press, 1999.

Schumann, Robert. *Symphony No. 2 in C Major*, opus 61 (1846).

Haydn, Franz Josef. *Symphony No. 104 in D Major* ("London") (1795).

Beethoven, Ludwig van; Jeitteles text translated by Thompson, Lynn. *An die ferne Geliebte*: Song Cycle for Voice and Piano, opus 98 (1816). Permission information available on copyright page.

Harrison, Robert Pogue. *Gardens: An Essay on the Human Condition*. Chicago: University of Chicago Press, 2008.

Goldman, William. *The Silent Gondoliers*. New York: Random House, 1983.

de la Mare, Walter. "All Hallows," in *Short Stories 1895–1926: Vol. 1*. London: Giles de la Mare Publishers, 1996.

West, Rebecca. *Black Lamb amd Grey Falcon: A Journey Through Yugoslavia*. New York: Penguin, 1994.

Tuchman, Barbara. *The Proud Tower: A Portrait of the World Before the War*, 1890–1914. New York: Macmillan, 1966.

Berg, Alban. *Violin Concerto* (1934–1935).

Rachmaninoff, Sergei. *Rhapsody on a Theme of Paganini* (1934–1935).

Vaughan Williams, Ralph. *The Lark Ascending* (1924); *Symphony No. 4* (1934).

Harbison, John. *Ulysses: A Ballet in Two Acts* (1983).

Celan, Paul; translated by Felstiner, John. *Selected Poems and Prose*. New York: Norton, 2000.

Schnackenberg, Gjertrud. *The Throne of Labdacus: A Poem*. New York: Farrar, Straus and Giroux, 2001.

Pessoa, Fernando; translated by Zenith, Richard. *Fernando Pessoa & Co.: Selected Poems*. New York: Grove, 1998.

Rilke, Rainer Maria; translated by Snow, Edward. *Duino Elegies*. New York: North Point Press, 2000.

Carson, Anne. *The Beauty of the Husband: A Fictional Essay in 29 Tangos*. New York: Random House, 2002.

Oliver, Mary. *American Primitive*. New York: Little, Brown, 1983.

Moss, Howard. *Rules of Sleep*. New York: Atheneum, 1984.

Springsteen, Bruce. *Born to Run* (1975).

Brahms, Johannes; Schiller text translated by Ezust, Emily. *Nänie* (1881). Permission information available on copyright page.

Rembrandt. *Gottes Verheißung an Abraham* (*God's Promise to Abraham*). Permission information available on copyright page.

Spektor, Regina. *Soviet Kitsch* (2004).

48954243R00108

Made in the USA
Middletown, DE
02 October 2017